DO YOU REMEMBER WHEN...

IN FAYETTE COUNTY, PA

By

VICTORIA DUTKO LEONELLI

Technical Editors:

Beth Bubonovich and Linda Jennings

Copyright © 2007 by Victoria Dutko Leonelli
ISBN 978-0-9796730-0-9
First Edition Printed in 2007
Second Edition Reprinted in 2008
Published by Victoria Dutko Leonelli
LCCN -2007903405
Printed in the United States

Marie Joseph Paul Yves Roch Gilbert du Motier, the Marquis de

Lafayette, Fayette County's namesake was one of the greatest patriots during the American Revolution.

On the cover-

The Fayette County Bar Association made it an annual event to retreat to the mountains for a day of relaxation. The lawyers forgot about anxious clients and legal tangles and played cards, tossed balls, pitched horseshoes and arm wrestled. They enjoyed a delicious chicken dinner and drank cold ale. There was also an exhilarating swimming contest at Seaton's Lake. These are some of the lawyers and their friends present at the 1894 gathering held at Washington Springs: T.R. Wakefield, R.W. Dawson, Ira E. Partridge, J.C. Work, W.G. Guiler, Nathaniel Ewing, Luke K. Frasher, S.L. Mestrezat, W.J. Johnson, Edward Campbell, E.D. Fulton, J.Q. Swearingen, D.M. Hertzog, James R. Cray, W.C. McKean, J.M. Oglevee, R.F. Hopwood, R.E. Umbel, A. Plumer Austin, Geo. B. Jefferies, W.W. Parshall, W.A. Hogg, Paoli S. Morrow, H.F. Detweiler, R.P. Kennedy, Chas. Kefover, D.W. McDonald, J.G. Carroll, Alex. Belt and Daniel Reynolds. (Mick Gallis collection.)

Mount Vernon Furnace is located in Bullskin Township on a narrow terrace and small stream near the head of Mountz Creek. This furnace was constructed by Isaac Meason, the Fayette County Iron Master around 1795. Meason built this furnace for his son Isaac. The Furnace was rebuilt around 1801. These folks are getting an inside view of the furnace as well as a close up look at the inscription "MT VN 1801" which was inscribed on an iron lintel above the main opening of the furnace. The Bullskin Historical Society is in support of preserving this important Fayette County historical landmark. (Author's collection.)

Order of Red Men and Degree of Pocahontas, please see page 25. (Patricia Dailey and Walter "Buzz" Storey & Polly Storey collection.)

Fourth of July celebrations have been a special occasion when families and friends gather to honor our country. Men, women and children worked very hard during the early days and this "time out" and customary celebration was well deserved. A traditional celebration such as this one would be a time for families to wave and display the American flag while they enjoyed a picnic lunch in a park or a country field while they breathed some cool fresh air. (Author's collection.)

No one was injured during an early morning fire that destroyed six structures and badly damaged some old and new public school buildings in Fayette City in January of 1910. Fire departments from several neighboring towns arrived on a special train and by trolley to help extinguish the flames. (Author's collection.)

ACKNOWLEDGMENTS

I would like extend my appreciation to my friends, Beth Bubonovich and Linda Jennings for their expert knowledge and wonderful advice; their commitment and dedication to this production was a great inspiration. My sincere gratitude is extended to the following individuals, organizations, businesses and institutions for their part in making this book a reality: Sandra L. Michotte, Interim Administrator, Uniontown Public Library; Christy Fusco, former Head Librarian, Uniontown Public Library; the Uniontown Public Library Board of Directors; Uniontown Public Library staff members; Friends of the Uniontown Public Library; McGarvey's One Hour Photo; Graphic Designer, Michelle Georgiana.

To Mark O'Keefe, editor of the Herald Standard, and the newspaper staff-past and present-my thanks to you for publishing informative articles about our rich local history. The Uniontown newspapers are a vital resource and have been preserved on microfilm for research purposes. The newspapers were an integral part of my research in acquiring historical facts to compliment the images in this book.

The following friends, family members and institutions contributed to this project by sharing images or by offering technical assistance: Joseph C. Alexander, Jr., Joseph Borytsky, William G. Brown, Beth & Mark Bubonovich, John Carom, Joan Carr, Charles & Mary Cluss, Adele Alexander Congelio, Patricia Dailey, Connie Sante Dutko, Ken Frye, Jr., Fayette County Historical Society, Mick Gallis, Michelle Georgiana, David Gratz, the Haky family, Linda Jennings, Anthony Keefer, Connie Kikta, Franklin V. La Cava, Curt Lehman, Patty Lint of the Tri-Town Historical Society, Rev. Peter Malik, Janice Mancuso, Carol Dutko Marshaus, Bob & Becky Wilhelm McGarvey, Tom Merryman, Sandra L. Michotte, Rita Foriska Miller, Renee Dutko Mueller, Bettie C. O'Neil, A. Patrick Pallini, Pierce family, Clinton Piper, Joanne Politano, Harry Porter, David Priest, Ed & Sally Reed, Charles Rohrer, Katie Sepkovic, Anita Shaffer, Kathy Smitley, Polly Storey, Jennifer Sterbutzel, Alfred H. Tewell, Johnny Vass, Dan Visnauskus, Western Pennsylvania Conservancy, Dale "Chilly" Williams, Betty O. Wilson, William R. Wilson, Bill & Lois Wolfersberger, and Margaret Cottom Young.

To my husband, Armand, and my children, Toni and Armand, Jr., thank you for your patience and understanding while I pursued this project.

And a special remembrance for those who have since passed away and who each shared my interest in preserving our county's history- William A. Balsley, Armond Gatts, Sol Michael, Jaci Roby, Jerome "Jerry" Storey, Walter "Buzz" Storey and Janice Childs Ward.

This book is dedicated to all of our friends and family members who are no longer with us –Vicki

Professor Elwood Heyser taught Uniontown Public School's music appreciation class. To the right of Professor Heyser is Nan Clark Allen who later became J. Searight Marshall's wife. The school was located where the Central School Building in Uniontown is presently located. The students were privileged to have a rather famous maestro giving them voice lessons and teaching them to play string instruments. Heyser's first composition was "The Swallow." He composed more than 1200 anthems and thirty-six complete cantatas. Today you may find sheet music attributed to Elwood Heyser. (Bettie C. O'Neil collection.)

I would like to thank the following individuals and businesses for their support in helping me to preserve our local history and making Do You Remember When ...possible.

Platinum Level

In Memory of Orville Eberly
From Carolyn and Gerald Blaney

In Memory of Leonelli and Dutko Ancestors
From the Leonelli Family

Silver Level

Elouise R. Eberly

Linda L. Jennings

Ruth Kikta Smoot

In Honor of Connie Sante Dutko
From Reneé Dutko Mueller

In Honor of the Lewis and Mary Lee Winston
Ford Family
From Oscar L. Sims

In Memory of Saul Swimmer
From Wolford and Lenore Swimmer

Gold Level

Gilbert M. Thompson

In Memory of Nelson and Bubonovich
Ancestors
From Mark and Beth Bubonovich

In Honor of Dolores Sante Cosgrove
From Bill, Paula, Lea, Tris and Will

In Memory of Armand and Elinor Kikta
Leonelli
From Armand, Toni and Armand, III

In Memory of Andrew and Sophie Wovas
From Edward and Harriet Wovas

Bronze Level

O. C. Cluss Lumber Co.

Davis & Davis
Attorneys at Law

Jan and Faye Ann Kikta

Table of Contents

Introduction

If you enjoy reminiscing about the good old days or are fascinated with the past, this pictorial history is a vehicle that you can use to travel back in time. It is filled with nostalgic images of people and places that once existed here in Fayette County. So much of our great country's early history began here and some of the photographs were selected to give you insight into that earlier time; others were chosen purely to provide an entertaining, lighthearted look at the past. I hope that you find viewing this collection and reading the descriptions both pleasurable and informative.

As you journey through the pages you will see dark clouds of smoke billowing out of the coke ovens of Fayette County and be aware of what life was like in a coal mining patch. You will be at hand at harvest time when the apple cider was just pressed. You will attend centennial celebrations, ride the streetcars to and from work, swim in the popular pools, and climb to the top of the White Rocks. You will march along the streets with thousands of others to celebrate the homecoming of our soldiers. You can stand alongside bargain hunters in a department store filled with wall-to-wall shoppers or walk past the home of a former princess. You will become part of a community where everyone knows everyone else.

Some of these photographic treasures have come out of attics, trunks and old cardboard boxes where they had been tucked away for many, many years. Others have graced the living rooms of their owners in frames or albums. A few of the images in this book are quite rare and have never before been published. I extend my sincere gratitude to all the individuals who unselfishly permitted me to borrow their prized photographs and share them with you. But I am most appreciative of the photographers, both amateur and professional, who had the foresight to capture the essence of everyday life and history making events many years ago.

I am hopeful that you, too, will take photographs of your neighborhood, your family reunion, your automobile, family members in their new clothes, a parade, your school, your church, your pet or your place of employment and preserve them for the future. These subjects may seem unimportant or mundane at the moment but the 'good old days' of the future are the days we are living now.

If you have photographs that you would like to share with the public but are reluctant to part with them, technology allows them to be reproduced without the risk of loss or damage to the originals. You may loan your photographs to the library to be digitally scanned; the originals will be returned promptly. All the images gathered during the last several years for this project have been preserved on CD-ROM and donated to the Uniontown Public Library for future reference.

If you are interested in purchasing copies of any of the photographs published in this book that are not copyrighted, you may contact me at 4 Connor Street, Uniontown, Pennsylvania 15401 or genealeo@atlanticbb. net for more information.

Sincerely,

Victoria Dutko Leonelli

Chapter 1
Fayette's Rich History

Rock carvings known as petroglyphs were found on a high bluff on the Horner Farm in Luzerne Township overlooking the Monongahela River. The large smooth rock was marked with the images of both hoglike and birdlike creatures, footprints of squirrels, a clawed animal, a bison, handprints and footprints and some other symbols. Posing on the rock are, left to right, three Carter brothers from Fredricktown, Pa., George Denny, Richard Oliver Denny, George Covert Denny, Mary Elizabeth Denny (Mrs. J. W. Farquhar) and Caroline Denny (Mrs. W. R. Tissue). In 1902 the petroglyphs were dynamited by farmer Joseph Harper who was angry with trespassers flocking to view the carvings. (Uniontown Public Library collection.)

David Gilmour Blythe was married to Julia Keffer who tragically passed away within one year of their marriage. He fell into a melancholy state and lived a precarious life from that time on. During the five years he resided in Uniontown, Blythe created some of his most ambitious works, carving both the statue of Lafayette as well as the raven that is proudly displayed at the Uniontown Public Library. He also painted The Great Moving Panorama of the Alleghenies, satirical political paintings and lovely portraits. Collectors of Blythe's art enjoy the challenge of identifying lost examples of his paintings, as he did not always sign his artwork. (Uniontown Public Library collection.)

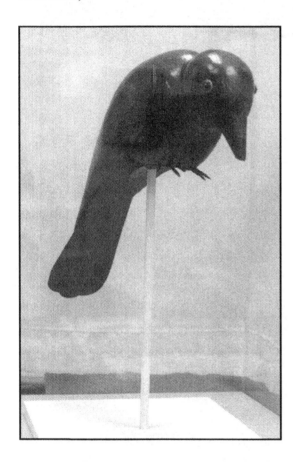

Working in the Old West School House on South Street in Uniontown in 1847, talented genre artist David Gilmour Blythe carved this statue of Lafayette out of poplar planks. It originally was mounted on the steeple of our county's third courthouse. The 8-feet, 2-inches tall statue of the Revolutionary War hero has been repainted a few times and moved to various locations. The eccentric artist's creation was even part of an exhibit at the Smithsonian. (*Herald-Standard*.)

Professor John Alfred Brashear was known throughout the scientific world as a distinguished astronomer and respected manufacturer of astronomical instruments. Brashear was born in Brownsville on November 24, 1840. His ancestors had settled in Brownsville in 1775, and his great-grandfather married a sister of Thomas and Basil Brown, founders of that town. (*Hart's Three Towns.*)

The Brashear House in Brownsville, birthplace of Astronomer J. A. Brashear, was kept by Basil Brashear and afterwards by James Searight. Lafayette was entertained here during his famous visit to America in 1825. He spoke to the citizens of the town from the doorway of this once prominent hostelry. (Mick Gallis collection.)

Nemacolin Castle in Brownsville is listed on the National Register of Historic Places. The name Nemacolin originates from the Native American leader in the district during the pre-Revolutionary War era. This impressive two-story dwelling was built around Jacob Bowman's trading post on the approximate site of Old Fort Burd. Jacob Bowman, a pioneer settler, was appointed by George Washington in 1789 to serve as Brownsville's first postmaster. The castle has a fascinating history and is opened for guided tours. (*Herald-Standard.*)

Do You Remember When...

On April 12, 1846 Fayette County Commissioners contracted with Samuel Bryan, Jr. of Harrisburg to build a new courthouse. The structure was built in the Greek-revival style with a large four-faced town clock mounted near the octagon-shaped belfry. Blythe's statue of Lafayette stood atop its spire. This courthouse opened in 1847. (Uniontown Public Library collection.)

An infamous character in Fayette County's past was William "Crazy Billy" Stanford who was incarcerated for a disturbance at a home in Nicholson Township and then later convicted for the murder of his cellmate. Crazy Billy became friends with the sheriff and his family, gaining him the right to roam freely throughout the prison and the courthouse, shown in the bottom photo. Prison officials considered Crazy Billy to be their mascot. According to legend, Crazy Billy's spirit continued to walk the halls of the courthouse after his death. Thousands of people have been buried in Oak Grove cemetery, but Crazy Billy has the most unique grave marker, made from one of the original columns of the second Fayette County Courthouse, built in 1847. The courthouse proved inadequate and was later torn down. The broken cement column was salvaged by a friend who placed it upon the final resting place of William Stanford – Crazy Billy, January 26, 1886. (Rev. Peter Malik collection.)

This is the earlier prison where Crazy Billy was held and committed murder against his cellmate. (Walter "Buzz" Storey collection.)

The Meason House was built in 1802 by Isaac Meason, Sr., the richest man in Fayette County. At one time Meason owned a forge, an iron furnace, a grist mill and two saw mills and 6400 acres of land in and around Dunbar Township. Meason was the first to manufacture iron in this county. The Meason House wasn't typical of the times. The mansion stood out from what was mostly unsettled wilderness scattered with log cabins. The limestone Georgian mansion resembled homes of the wealthy in England and early Philadelphia. Architect and craftsman Adam Wilson traveled to Mount Braddock from England to design the mansion. When Isaac Meason passed away January 23, 1818, he left his heirs great wealth along with 20,000 acres of the best coal lands in western Pennsylvania. (Uniontown Public Library collection.)

The land on which the Meason House was built was once known as the Gist Plantation. In 1753 Christopher Gist had acquired this piece of desirable land that was being claimed by both Virginia and Pennsylvania in a boundary dispute. It is believed that during the 1800s this property was used as a stop along the Underground Railroad. The Meason House property and its intriguing history make the list as one of Fayette County's greatest landmarks. (Fayette County Historical Society.)

Do You Remember When...

Henry Beeson, a Virginia Quaker, was the founder of Uniontown. Beeson was on his way to Kentucky when he discovered this fertile land below the Allegheny Mountains and chose to make it his home. Beeson laid out the town of Union on July 4, 1776 and posted fifty-four lots for sale through a town lottery. He donated the land east of the courthouse on a gently sloping hillside for a public cemetery. Six-feet tall with dark eyes and an intelligent appearance, Beeson was mannerly and mild and known to be quite generous. Henry Beeson moved to Mt. Pleasant, Ohio in 1804 where he died of paralysis in 1819. His wife Mary Martin Beeson also passed away there in 1821. (James Hadden.)

Henry Beeson purchased a tract of land from pioneer Thomas Douthet. Beeson built his family a magnificent home on a plot of seventy acres. The site he selected was near an elegant spring on a hillside overlooking a vast tract east of the old Catawba Trail. Rich red clay on the property was used to form bricks utilized in the construction of the mansion. The bricks gave the house a checkered appearance. (James Hadden.)

In 1772 Henry Beeson chose the sites for two grist mills. Beeson's mills were built in prominent and convenient locations for people to conduct business. The first was north of Gallatin Avenue where the Redstone Creek provided a water source for the mill. This was also between the Youghiogheny and Monongahela Rivers that provided river travel for families who settled nearby. The second location was to the west near the site of the Titlow Hotel. The town was referred to early on as Beesontown. As families moved here and businesses and industries were developed, the area evolved into the city of Union-town. (Uniontown Public Library collection.)

Do You Remember When...

Jacob Beeson purchased about 251 acres in Beesontown from his brother Henry and called his new homestead Mt. Vernon. The Beesons, a Quaker family, lived in a small rustic cabin when the area was mostly wilderness. It was located where the home of the Princess of Thurn and Taxis later stood. Today the Mt. Vernon Towers is located on this lot. Jacob Beeson built a splendid mansion on the nearby hill at South Mt. Vernon Avenue and West Main Street. For years the Mount Vernon Inn and hotel buildings surrounded Jacob's house so completely that passersby rarely noticed it. The section known today as Five Corners is actually one of Uniontown's most historical areas. In this sketch, Jacob appears quite serious as he gazes towards his house and land. (James Hadden.)

Jacob Beeson's mansion house can be seen on the right in this early photograph of the west end of Uniontown. It remained in the family for a few years after Jacob's death and then the home passed through the hands of some very prominent families in the community. Lucius W. Stockton occupied the house for a time and referred to it as "Ben Lomond." Stockton operated the oldest and largest stagecoach line along the National Road; his coaches delivered the mail. The Gilmores and Kennedys were associated with this mansion as well. Jacob's mansion was razed in 2005 to make way for a new business. It took a crew of men with a huge bulldozer to level this sturdy house almost two hundred years after it was built. The Princess of Thurn and Taxis lived in the former Veach mansion shown on the far left side of this picture. (Author's collection, top. Uniontown Public Library collection, middle.)

Do You Remember When...

This lovely lady is posing next to the "post office" at White Rocks. The hole in the rock served as a mailbox for those wanting to trade messages. Some people would also carve their initials in the rocks or write messages directly on the boulders. (Uniontown Public Library collection.)

In August of 1810, Polly Williams, an attractive young servant girl from New Salem, was pushed off a cliff by her fiancé, Phillip Rogers. Four children picking berries near the foot of the White Rocks found her lifeless body. The steep outcropping is located about three miles east of the Hopwood-Fairchance Road. Polly's body was carried to the old Moses Nixon Tavern (later referred to as Polly Williams House) at North Main Street and Elm in Fairchance. After the coroner's report was made public, it was determined that her fall was not an accident. Rogers had tossed rocks on top of Polly's battered body. A sensational and seemingly unfair trial took place. The Rogers family hired Senator James Ross, a wealthy attorney from Pittsburgh. Polly's family had moved from the area in 1808 prior to her death, but it was unlikely that her family would have had the means to secure legal representation. Rogers never admitted to the murder and was acquitted but Polly Williams' memory lived on. A poignant epitaph taken from a ballad was written on her gravestone. The Polly Williams Sunday School Class was named for her at the Little White Rock Church. A novel entitled *White Rocks* was published in 1865 by Ashbel Fairchild Hill of German Township and a chapter in the book *Rose and Elza* by Elizabeth Curstead tell the tragic tale. Students, historians and tourists are still drawn to the White Rocks and to Polly's final resting place. (Alfred H. Tewell collection.)

Carpenter Hugh Graham was an Irish immigrant of Scottish parentage who journeyed on foot from Philadelphia to Pittsburgh in only six days. Carrying the tools of his trade with him, he proceeded on to Fayette County where he met and married Margaret Black. Hugh Graham built numerous fine houses in the area, but is best known for the stone addition to Albert Gallatin's house at Friendship Hill. Tradition says Native Americans who once camped on this land referred to it as "Friendly Hill" and that ensuing settlers on this property called it Friendship Hill. (A. Patrick Pallini collection.)

Sophia Alegre was looking forward to becoming the wife of the prominent Albert Gallatin. Gallatin brought his new bride to the original brick house that he built at New Geneva in June of 1789, only to lay her to rest in a lonely grave a few months later. It is said that poor Sophia died of loneliness. Her mother was against Sophia's marriage to Gallatin. Although Friendship Hill was fit for royalty in those days, it was located in the wilderness of southwestern Pennsylvania. Legends state that Sophia's spirit walks the vast estate and has been seen gazing out of the window as if watching for her dear husband's return from a distant business or political meeting. (Uniontown Public Library collection.)

Albert Gallatin established the first glass factory west of the Alleghenies. He is well remembered in this area for founding the town of New Geneva in 1794, but Gallatin holds a prominent place in American political history. He was a member of the convention that revised our state constitution in 1789 and was soon elected to the U.S. Senate but he was not permitted to take that seat because he was born in Switzerland. Gallatin was repeatedly elected to the House of Representatives where he was allowed to serve. In 1801 he was appointed Secretary to the Treasury and was one of the most important dignitaries in bringing about the Treaty of Ghent. Albert Gallatin will always be remembered for his inspirational speech welcoming Lafayette to America. He retired from public life in 1828. (Uniontown Public Library collection.)

During the 1800s, the prominent Oliphant family of Fairchance owned Liberty Hall, an impressive country home built near the early Native American path known as the Cherokee or Catawba Trail that once led from the North to the South. Liberty Hall had its own stables and a private racetrack for the purebred horses that were boarded there. The Oliphant's grand estate became the setting for elite social events of the period. (Uniontown Public Library collection.)

Fort Gaddis was an early frontier fort built by Colonel Thomas Gaddis who was third in command in Col. William Crawford's ill-fated expedition against the Indians in 1782. The fort is located in South Union Township off Morgantown Road in the location of the Catawba Trail. Basil A. Brownfield owned the fort years later. The fort had been unoccupied for many years before this picture was taken on October 30, 1909. S. E. Wadsworth, a Civil War veteran is in this photograph standing close to the historical landmark tablet with Mrs. Brownfield and Basil's daughter. Wadsworth was married to Sarah Brownfield and they resided at Sycamore. (Walter "Buzz" Storey collection.)

A well-known mill was located in Smithfield a few yards to the left of present-day Ruble Road just before crossing the countryside bridge at Reese's Wholesale. Jacob Ruble purchased the mill in 1871 and operated it until 1899. Farmers would wait in line at this popular mill to have their grain ground into flour for their kitchens and feed for their livestock. The mill had a very long history that dated back to Meshack Davis and Jesse Evans, original owners. The property would change hands many times through the years. (Uniontown Public Library collection.)

Do You Remember When...

THE OLD COOK MANSION WHERE PRESIDENT GEO. WASHINGTON

Colonel Edward Cook was the original owner of the land situated along the Monongahela River twelve miles from Brownsville that became Fayette City. This area in Washington Township was once the site of a Native American village. Colonel Cook called the town he established in 1800, Freeport; from 1825 to 1854 it was known as Cookstown. Cook was prominent in county, state and military matters and a dynamic leader during the Whiskey Insurrection. Colonel Cook's house neaFayette City was built in the style of an eastern Pennsylvania farmhouse. (Mick Gallis collection.)

Norval Willson Greenland was one of Uniontown's most respected citizens. He was born in an old log cabin in 1824, the son of Abner and Jane Thompson Greenland. Norval Greenland and his father became well known for their pieces of handmade pottery. He built up the area where the old log cabin once stood, later known as Commercial Block on Morgantown and Church Streets, and had his pottery business there. In 1874 he married Sarah Laughead and they resided on Gallatin Avenue. Norval Greenland passed away August 23, 1903, leaving his wife and a large family. (Uniontown Public Library collection.)

"Aunt Janie" Johnson lived to be ninety-nine years of age and died in the house in which she was born. Jane was the daughter of Abner and Elizabeth Vance Springer, owners of a 147-acre original land patent. Even though she was a child at the time, she could clearly remember the year 1825 when Lafayette visited Fayette County. One of her favorite recollections was stirring a large cauldron of apple butter with a long-handled wooden stick. She lived a modest life, was good-natured and charitable and loved children. Mrs. Isaac (Jane) Johnson was the oldest resident of Uniontown when she died in 1920. (Uniontown Public Library collection.)

The Springer House was built around 1817 on land warranted to Levi Springer. The two-story, fourteen-room house is nearly twice the size of others built in southwestern Pennsylvania at that time. Some historians have said that it was intended as a tavern along the National Road but there was a change of plans and the road wasn't built in front of the house. Genealogists say that the home had many rooms in order to accommodate a large family. Bricks used in building it were formed and fired on the property. Porches stretched the length of the house front and back and on both

floors. The Springers farmed the property. One of the county home cemeteries is located on the original parcel of land. The Springer Homestead is on the National Register. (Uniontown Public Library collection.)

OL. CRAWFORD'S SPRING.

Colonel William Crawford was born in the Shenandoah Valley of Virginia and was a lifetime friend of George Washington. Crawford settled along the Youghiogheny River at Stuart's Crossing, now known as Connellsville. During the Revolution, Colonel Crawford was appointed by Washington to take command of Colonial troops on the frontier. After a disastrous battle in 1782 against the Indians, Crawford's troops were ambushed and Crawford was captured. He was taken to an Indian camp where the town of Upper Sandusky now stands. On the morning of July 7, 1782, Colonel Crawford was tied to a stake, tortured and burned. Colonel William Crawford is recognized as a great hero and soldier whose efforts were invaluable in developing and protecting the western border. (Uniontown Public Library collection.)

John Gibson, a business partner of Isaac Meason, settled in this part of the country around 1793. Gibson had an early gristmill, a forge and a sawmill and was associated with the building of the second blast furnace west of the Allegheny Mountains. Upon his death, John's sons, Thomas and Joseph, inherited much of their father's wealth. In 1870 the town of Gibsonville was laid out by one of Joseph Gibson's sons in part of Connellsville and eighteen houses were erected. During the early 19th century, Joseph had built a solid stone house that would stand for two centuries when other structures built around the same era could not. This historical house is

located on West Patterson Avenue facing South Arch Street. The Gibson House is in the process of being restored through the efforts of the Connellsville Area Historical Society, some government agencies and young people from the community. (Harry Porter collection.)

Do You Remember When...

These relics were found at Fort Necessity by a group accompanying McClelland Leonard who had hoped to donate the relics to the public library for a museum. Fifty-pound cannon balls, a hook, a bridle bit, a hatchet, large spikes and a pile of horseshoe nails were among the items found about two feet underground at the dig site. (Uniontown Public Library collection.)

General Edward Braddock and his group of British regulars and Virginia militiamen were sent to fight for control of this area. Braddock and his men laid out a road in the vast mountainous terrain that would bear his name but he is mostly remembered for the battle in which hundreds of his men died or were seriously wounded. Braddock, dressed for victory in an expensive gaudy uniform he helped to design, was mortally wounded and buried in the road to keep his crudely made coffin hidden from the French. (Uniontown Public Library collection.)

 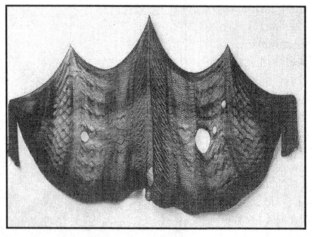

General Braddock's red silk sash worn at the time of his death in 1755 bears a hole and dark stain. It was displayed at the October 15, 1913 dedication of the monument erected at his grave. Miss Mary Spotswood Buchanan stayed at the Summit Inn after traveling on the B&O Railroad to bring the sash for the service. Both George Washington and General Zachary Taylor had owned the sash for a time. (Uniontown Public Library collection.)

This view of Fort Necessity was taken on July 4, 1904, the sesquicentennial anniversary of the beginning of the French and Indian War. Fort Necessity is indicated by the stripe of the bunting and the flag. The procession is passing from the National Road down the private drive to the grove where a speech is about to be presented. The French made their first attack from the location of the white house in the background. (Uniontown Public Library collection.)

The cornerstone at Fort Necessity was laid in 1854, the centennial anniversary of Washington's surrender there. Fort Necessity was designated as a National Battlefield Site by an Act of Congress in 1931. (Uniontown Public Library collection.)

A roughhewn cross on the mountainside marked the grave of M. Coulon de Jumonville or Sieur de Jumainville, a native of France and ensign during the French and Indian War. The French commander lost his life at age twenty-nine fighting against Col. George Washington and his troops. As a tribute to the French hero, this pastoral area in the mountains above Uniontown was named Jumonville. (Uniontown Public Library collection.)

The first meeting of the Whiskey Insurrection was held at the Black Horse Tavern on Front Street in Brownsville on July 29, 1791. The meeting place was originally Redstone Old Fort. The last public meeting of the Insurrection took place in the same building on August 28th and 29th in 1794. (Uniontown Public Library collection.)

The beautiful land on which the town of Perryopolis is situated caught the eye of George Washington who was on a surveying trip a short time before Braddock's expedition. Washington later acquired the land; some say he bought it from Colonel William Crawford who had already established it as his by a "tomahawk claim." Washington's Mill in Perryopolis was built upon part of the tract that once contained seventeen hundred acres. The mill could grind a bushel of corn in one minute, quite a feat in those early days. It was probably the first mill erected within the county. When Samuel Smith owned the mill he powered it with a steam engine. Although it has been rebuilt several times, the mill still remains as constructed under the direction of Washington. (Author's collection.)

Tom Fossit was a provincial soldier in the army during 1755. Fossit despised General Braddock after he witnessed the general strike his brother Joe Fossit with his sword. Sometimes Fossit claimed to have killed Braddock, at other times he denied the terrible deed. There was never enough evidence to prove or disprove his story. Tom Fossit lived to be 106 years old and left no heirs. His headstone once disappeared from the old graveyard north of Campground Road in Ohiopyle State Park but was recovered by a park ranger. For years the locals have placed a flag on his grave every Memorial Day. (Uniontown Public Library collection.)

In August of 1908, John Kennedy Lacock led a 130-mile Historical Pedestrian Expedition to rediscover the history and location of Braddock's Road. Lacock was accompanied by a group of historians, scholars and friends. During June and July of 1909, they took a second trip. James Hadden, local historian and talented photographer, was with them to capture the event with his camera. Ernest K. Weller of Washington, Pa. also took photographs. Lacock and his entourage took shelter at the Soldier's Orphan School and home at Jumonville and at the log cabins of friends who lived in the mountains. (Uniontown Public Library collection.)

Do You Remember When...

William Warnick of High House was a stonemason who also worked for the WPA during the Great Depression. Mr. Warnick couldn't recall why he began to sculpt this seven-feet tall Native American statue but he eventually created two of them. Warnick chiseled away for hours to make the colorful sandstone chips that were held together by cement on an iron frame. One of his creations greets guests at Ye Olde Inn on Route 119 North in Dunbar Township. The other kept vigil in front of Warnick's home along High House Road during the 1940s, generating a great deal of interest from passersby. (Rev. Peter Malik collection.)

Chapter 2
In the Community's Interest

The Degree of Pocahontas was a society formed in 1886 named for the renowned heroine in early American history. Pocahontas' brief life was a model of grace, virtue, integrity, generosity and friendship. The members of this organization dressed in authentic Native American costumes for their meetings. The male organization associated with this group was The Improved Order of Red Men. Sadie Wilson Rout, wife of Emmet Rout and daughter of Calvin and Margaret Wilson of Georges Township, was a member of the Fayette County branch of the Degree of Pocahontas. (Patricia Dailey collection.)

The late Walter "Buzz" Storey was one of Uniontown's greatest local historians and writers. A graduate of St. John's High School, Buzz attended Penn State University, the University of Wisconsin and Waynesburg College. At the age of 13, he worked as a newspaper carrier boy. Buzz became a writer and photographer with the local newspaper in 1940 and in 1954 he was named assistant editor of the *Morning Herald* and *Evening Standard*. A veteran of World War II, he won the state Better Writing competition and led team efforts that resulted in two Associated Press National Citations and three American Legion state first place awards for veterans' news items. He rose to the position of editor of the *Herald Standard* and authored a local historical column. Buzz wrote two local history books and edited the video *Uniontown Unique*. Storey Square next to the State Theatre was named for him. Buzz modestly loaned this image to the author and was pleased to know it would be published. (Walter "Buzz" Storey collection.)

Taking a well-deserved break, these *News Standard* carriers are enjoying ice cream cones compliments of Hagan Ice Cream. Regardless of the weather they delivered the newspapers every morning and evening on foot; taking them by automobile was unheard of in the 1930s. Another part of the job was to sell the papers to pedestrians on downtown streets. (*News Standard*, 1933.)

Do You Remember When...

Mabel at the Fountain once stood at the intersection of Morgantown, South and Church Streets. The Women's Christian Temperance Unions and the "Y" of Fayette County donated the public drinking fountain to Uniontown. It was unveiled July 3, 1896 during Uniontown's centennial celebration. Josiah V. Thompson accepted the gift on behalf of the community. Mabel weighed 3500 pounds and stood 14-feet high. It was built by J. W. Fist of York, Pa. The water poured out from four horse heads and a dozen drinking cups were chained to the pedestal for the public's use. Humans, horses and dogs all shared the cool water that spouted from the Grecian-looking statue. Around 1919 the fountain was taken to Confluence and, regrettably, it was melted down during a World War II scrap drive. A horse head from the fountain is the one and only relic known to exist today and may be seen at the Uniontown Public Library. (Uniontown Public Library collection, top right. Walter "Buzz" Storey collection, top left and bottom left)

The American Legion Lafayette Post had 620 members when they held a housewarming in March of 1920 for their new home on Gallatin Avenue. The former Lindsey residence was painted and cleaned from top to bottom for the occasion. Years later a celebration dinner was held at the Legion for the veterans who marched in the 1946 Victory parade. (Author's collection.)

Prominent Fayette County businessman John Gilmore lived in a brick and stone mansion in South Union Township that had a picturesque view of the city and the mountains. The house remained in the Gilmore family until the Knights of Columbus acquired it in December of 1955. When plans were made for the huge Uniontown Mall complex, the mansion was demolished. (Knights of Columbus.)

Eccentric land developer John Brown built an elaborate mansion with crystal chandeliers and polished marble floors on a 13-acre estate in North Union Township in 1927. Some say there were once glass floors and two-way mirrors within the mansion. On the grounds were splendid gardens, basketball and tennis courts, a cement pool, stone towers, fishponds, stables, and a smaller seven-room house. The Greek Orthodox Church Charities bought the estate for $44,000 at auction on October 18, 1958. Today, the Knights of Columbus is located there. (Pierce family collection.)

The members of the Grand Army of the Republic held a reunion during June of 1927. Civil War veterans and other invitees attended a reception at the White Swan and an old-fashioned ox roast at Bailey Park. A parade with about 2,000 visiting delegates of the G.A.R. moved east on Main Street from the West End. One hundred boy scouts and girl scouts tossed flower petals along the parade route. Thousands crowded the streets, waving American flags. All of the local military organizations and bugle and drum corps participated. Musicians played national hymns and patriotic music, creating an atmosphere befitting the men that served our country during the Civil War. (Author's collection.)

Local Boy Scouts planned a hike in the 1930s to the Whyel scouting lodge at Jumonville. The scouts met at North Union High School and then hiked along Coolspring Road into the mountains. Each scout carried sufficient food and blankets and brought along pencil and paper and a camera to record what they would learn from their nature studies. The scouts attended services at the Whyel Chapel on Sunday morning. (*News Standard.*)

The Brownsville-Uniontown Branch of the NAACP held a celebration marking the anniversary of the organization's founding in 1909. Fayette County's NAACP hosted prominent African-American Bishop Stephen Gill Spottswood of Washington, D.C. who was associated with the "Fight for Freedom" program. (Author's collection.)

The Braddock Park Association held an elaborate celebration on October 15, 1913 after the Colonial Dames unveiled the monument erected in memory of Major General Edward Braddock. Chairman Edgar Hackney and James C. Work, John D. Carr, Charles Seaton, J. Searight Marshall and James Hadden were members of the Invitation Committee. Association member George Titlow invited the dignitaries to a luncheon at his hotel that afternoon.

Distinguished guests were later treated to a champagne toast and fancy dinner at the Summit Inn. A toast was made to the King and the President of the United States. Local historian James Hadden was commended for his efforts in acquiring the monument. Those in attendance heard speeches from Lieutenant Sir A. E. Codrington and the Honorable Philander Knox. At the conclusion of the speeches the men sang, "For He's a Jolly Good Fellow" and the Pennsylvania state song. The ladies in attendance were served dinner in the women's parlor room at the Summit, while the men enjoyed their meal in a room set just for them. Mrs. F. M. Semans, Mrs. R. E. Umbel, Mrs. John Core, Mrs. J. C. Work and Mrs. John Lynch were the organizers of the ladies social activities and dinner. (Uniontown Public Library collection.)

Do You Remember When...

Sarah Boyd Cochran, one of the wealthiest women ever to live in Fayette County, built Linden Hall in Dawson around 1912. Overlooking the scenic Youghiogheny River, this palatial mansion is perched on a six-hundred foot bluff in Saint James Park. Mrs. Cochran, widow of coal magnate Phillip Galley Cochran, was known nationally for her philanthropy, notably donations to many churches and colleges. When she learned of the sinking of the Titanic, Mrs. Cochran traveled to New York to assist her niece who had been onboard. She is locally regarded for the Phillip G. Cochran Memorial Methodist Episcopal Church that she had erected in memory of her husband. (Author's collection, left. Tri-Town Historical Society, right.)

Do You Remember When...

When the Uniontown Hospital opened its doors in 1903, a horse-drawn ambulance was still used to transport the sick or injured to and from the hospital. The skillful driver would train the horse to run as fast as possible. If an accident occurred outside the city, the ambulance would make the pickup at the railroad station. It must have been very sad for the faithful driver of the horse-drawn ambulance to be replaced by the automobile. (Author's collection.)

George C. Scott is about to pull out in one of the Keystone Fire Company's older horse-drawn hose wagons. Prior to 1915, fires were extinguished by manpower and pump machines like this one. (Uniontown Firemen booklet.)

The Fayette County Courthouse on East Main Street towers above the city. The courthouse was built in 1891-92 of gray sandstone that was quarried in Fayette County. The oak used in the courthouse was grown here, the iron used was rolled at a nearby mill and all of the bricks were molded right here in the county as well. The architectural style is known as Richardsonian Romanesque and is similar to the courthouse in Pittsburgh. Edward M. Butz and William Kaufmann of Pittsburgh were the architects. Blythe's statue of Lafayette is located in the lobby of the County Building that adjoins the courthouse. (Author's collection.)

The Bridge of Sighs is the most extraordinary feature of the Fayette County Prison. A stoned archway built in 1902 spans the alleyway, connecting the prison with Courtroom Number One of the county's courthouse. Prisoners could be moved back and forth without ever going outside. Executions and hangings continued in the jail yard until 1914. (Uniontown Public Library collection.)

Cooley Gang members Sam Yeager, Jack Ramsey, Brent Frye, Frank Cooley and Jack Cooley posed for this picture during the 1890s. According to legend, the Cooley Gang terrorized the residents around the Fairchance and Smithfield areas, torturing their victims before robbing them of their possessions. A favorite hiding place for their loot was Delaney's Cave, also known as Robber's Den. Some of the members were eventually apprehended and sent to jail while others were shot on the spot. In October 1892 Sheriff George A. McCormick gunned down Frank Cooley, the leader of this notorious gang of outlaws. (Uniontown Public Library collection.)

The Lodge members who organized St. John the Baptist Greek Catholic Church of Uniontown are pictured around 1910 in front of the former Madison Academy where the church now stands. The author's great-grandfather Joseph Dutko was a founding member and is standing towards the center of the third row back. (St. John the Baptist Anniversary booklet.)

This is a striking view looking eastward at Saint John the Baptist Greek Church on East Main Street. The church was built in 1911 and the congregation at that time was made up primarily of immigrants from Podkarpatska Rus' and eastern Slovakia. (Uniontown Public Library collection.)

Brothers Rudy and Ted Dutko pose at
St. John the Evangelist Roman Catholic
Church in 1935 with their sister Cecilia
Dutko who is a celebrant of her First
Holy Communion. The author's father
Rudy Dutko is the young boy holding
the prayer book. (Carol Dutko Marshaus
collection.)

It is sad to see an old church torn from its foundation even to
build a larger more modern one. This is the Presbyterian Church
in Uniontown after being partly demolished. This was the third
structure here, built in April of 1860 at a cost of ten thousand
dollars. The church had magnificent frescoes, well-built wooden
pews and stained glass windows. Repairs were made to the
windows around 1881. Rev. W.F. Hamilton was an early pastor
here. In January of 1894 ground was broken for a new church.
(Walter "Buzz" Storey collection.)

The Miracle Chimney at Collier Works was seen by thirty to
forty thousand persons during a week in June of 1935. The
spectators turned up to see the image of Christ that appeared
on a chimney of a small frame house and paid a fee of five
cents for children, twenty-five cents for adults, for admission
onto the property of Joseph Sterle. Five thousand visitors,
some from as far away as Florida, waited outside on just one
day. The Bishop was called in from Pittsburgh and announced
that the Church had temporarily taken over. They wanted
to make the house a public shrine. The Catholic Church
used the money collected to help pay off a large mortgage
on the Fairchance church building. (Walter "Buzz" Storey
collection.)

This is a rare image of the interior of the church McClelland Leonard purchased. The woodwork was made from the best hardwoods and the hand-blown lights added a special glow that was perfect for reading. The only sounds one could hear were footsteps and a whisper or two; talking aloud wasn't permitted. This building would be the home of the Uniontown Public Library for many years until a more modern library was built on Jefferson Street. (Uniontown Public Library collection.)

This young lady appreciates the quiet at the library where she can read her favorite poetry book. (Author's collection.)

Public library service in Uniontown dates back to 1912 when the Women's Civic League sponsored the Free Reading Room. Elizabeth Leonard took it over in 1915 and kept it going for more than a decade. The Civic League met in 1927 to arrange the purchase of the Methodist Protestant Church building on Church St. and Beeson Blvd. to use as a library. McClelland Leonard financed the endeavor and founded the Uniontown Public Library. (Walter "Buzz" Storey collection.)

Did you ever read *Captain Cut-Throat, The Dead Man's Knock or It Walks by Night*? These are just some of the popular works written by John Dickson Carr, a noted mystery writer. Carr was best known for his "locked room mysteries" in which the reader is encouraged to solve the puzzle before the solution is revealed. During his time in Fayette County, Carr lived in J. V. Thompson's skyscraper, the Fayette Bank building, and later at 52 South Mt. Vernon Avenue and 25 Ben Lomond Street. Carr, who was born in Uniontown in 1906, made numerous visits back to his birthplace. He was a childhood friend and neighbor of Judge Edward Dumbauld and cousin of the late Judge Philip O. Carr, both of Uniontown. The novelist and his wife escaped harm in 1940 during a real-life drama when a thousand-pound bomb demolished their new London home but left them uninjured. John Dickson Carr died at his South Carolina home in February 1977. (*Herald Standard.*)

On August 14th-17th, 1906, Connellsville held its centennial celebration, the most elaborate event in the history of the city. The President of the Centennial Association was Rockwell Marietta. The homes in Connellsville were decorated with flags and bunting. Hundreds of women, men and children from the community gathered on the lawn of the Carnegie Library dressed in their Sunday best. In 2006 Connellsville celebrated its bicentennial. (Author's collection.)

During the 1930s Mrs. H. D. (Jennie Leonard) Hutchinson was the supervisor of the Uniontown Free Public Library. Mrs. Hutchinson was a sister of McClelland Leonard. The Leonard family of Uniontown was instrumental in providing a permanent site for the adults and children in the community to read and learn in a comfortable environment. (*News Standard.*)

Do You Remember When...

The purpose of the Soldier's Orphan School was to provide food, clothing, education, musical training and recreation, as well as a temporary home to the children of those who fought in the Civil War. Not only did the school care for the children of those killed or disabled in battle, but they also provided the same services to children who were born to injured soldiers years after the war had ended. (Uniontown Public Library collection.)

Established in 1909 the McCrum Slavonic Missionary Training School instructed young women of foreign birth in Christian work. The original school was on Beeson Avenue before moving to the former estate of Captain A.C. Nutt. The captain and his mansion were the center of the high profile Duke-Nutt murder trial of the 1800s. The first superintendent of the Slavonic Training School was Elizabeth S. Davis, daughter of the Asbury Methodist Church minister who founded the Coke Mission, a Christian group that worked with the area's immigrants. Ms. Davis traveled to Bohemia to study the language and customs of the people. She brought several young women back with her and gave them an education at the school. After Elizabeth S. Davis retired as superintendent in 1922, the school became the McCrum Community Center under the supervision of the Women's Missionary Societies of the Pittsburgh Conference of the Methodist Church. (Anthony Keefer collection.)

Do You Remember When...

Prior to an enactment of the children's law in 1883, homeless and abandoned children between the ages of two and sixteen were placed in the Alms House or County Home. The Children's Aid Society sponsored a system to place children in foster homes. By 1940 the county paid a foster family or institution four dollars a week for board, ten to fifteen dollars annually for medical bills, and a twenty-five dollar per year clothing allowance. The Children's Home at 141 Oakland Avenue in Uniontown was one of several group homes for children in the county. (Janice Childs Ward collection.)

The Young Men's Christian Association has been in existence here since 1887. Community leaders met at the Methodist Protestant Church at the corner of Church Street and Beeson for the purpose of organizing the "Y." In 1921, the YMCA building was constructed for $100,000 at the corner of Peter Street and Gallatin Avenue. (*News Standard.*)

The stately brick four-story County Home along the National Road in South Union Township was originally the county's poor house. It was built on a tract of land purchased from Peter McCann in 1824 that was expanded with an adjoining tract bought from Alexander Turner in 1834. It eventually became a care facility for the seriously ill and the handicapped. Enough food was grown on the surrounding acres to feed the residents of the home. (Kathy Smitley collection.)

The debating team of 1929 at Dunbar Township High School in Leisenring earned their seventh straight championship and went on to the southwestern Pennsylvania competition. They had to beat both Connellsville and Uniontown in order to represent the county. Standing are debating team members Robert Fuller and Joseph Matuschak and seated are Mary M. Callahan, E.H. Hickman, the coach, and Grace Weaver. (Dunbar High School Yearbook.)

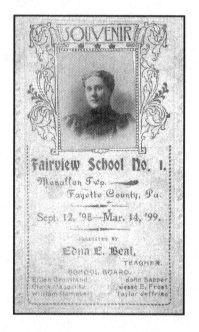

This celebration card is from the Fairview School in Menallen Township. The pupils attending Fairview in 1898-99 were Clayton Barnes, Springer Barnes, Myrtle Carter, Odale Carter, Leanor Colley, Clara Colley, Ethelburt Colley, Frank Colley, Keys Colley, Rachel Cramer, Albert Davis, Elsie Davis, Maggie Davis, Edna Davis, Haddie Gordon, Mary Gordon, James Gordon, Keys Graham, Myrtle Grimes, Lucy Grimes, Rena Hardin, Elza Helmick, Belle Jeffries, Lucie Jeffries, Lillie Krepps, Francis McVay, Blanche Shrum, Margaret Stewart, and Merle Todd. (Author's collection.)

Uniontown Senior High School had such a good academic reputation during the early 1900s that Waynesburg College would accept Uniontown graduates without having them take the usual entrance examinations. In 1916 the students at UHS voted between *The Dynamo, The Mirror or Maroon and White* as the name for the high school newspaper. *The Mirror* won. (U.H.S. Yearbook, 1922.)

World War I Army trucks are lined up for a community celebration near the home of prominent undertaker Joseph Haky of 139 West Fayette Street. Both Joseph and Stephen, Mr. Haky's sons, served our country during World War I, were honorably discharged and later became assistant undertakers at their family business. (Haky family collection.)

The World War I Doughboy statue at the Five Corners in Uniontown is one of many that were mass-produced after World War I. Our Doughboy was dedicated in 1936 and is cast in bronze. Today he is surrounded with flags, other statues, flowers and tablets engraved with historical information in what is now the George C. Marshall Memorial Park. The Marshall Foundation, local citizens and the VFW of Uniontown were instrumental in bringing about this patriotic tribute. (Haky family collection.)

Do You Remember When...

Participants filed by the Manos Theater on Main Street in a parade held July 4, 1946 in Uniontown to honor the veterans of World War II. About 1500 men and women who served in the military marched in full uniform accompanied by four bands. An estimated 25,000 enthusiastic parade goers turned out for the patriotic tribute. The national holiday celebration was a four-day event. (Uniontown Public Library collection.)

During World War II many factories like this one in Brownsville were taken over to manufacture machinery and tools that were needed for the war. (Uniontown Public Library collection.)

Uniontown Sr. High School students gathered as much metal as possible for the school's scrap drive in 1943. During World War II scrap metal was melted down and used for necessities like munitions. (U.H.S. Yearbook.)

Do You Remember When...

A devastating tornado touched down in the County in June of 1944, spewing about automobile hoods, brush, trees, rocks and other storm debris. The funnel-shaped cloud erratically passed over towns during the night, lasting about fifteen minutes and traveling within a one hundred-mile circle. William G. Brown had just returned home on a furlough during WWII and recalls the headlines comparing the twister's damage to a war zone. These photographs were taken after the tornado passed through the Smithfield area. The Paul School was directly in the path of destruction when the tornado crossed the New Geneva Road and tore into Smithfield. Ten people were injured and twelve homes were damaged, including the Leroy Conn property. (William G. Brown collection.)

Two of Uniontown's most famous sons, Chief of Staff General George C. Marshall and Colonel Paul H. Griffith, National Commander of the American Legion, showed their admiration and respect for each other for contributions they each made to our country during war times. Griffith is presenting General Marshall with a lifetime membership into the Lafayette Post No. 51. General George C. Marshall was an Army Chief of Staff, served as both Secretary of State and Secretary of Defense, authored the Marshall Plan and won the prestigious Nobel Peace Prize. (*The Lafayette.*)

Paul H. Griffith served his country during both World Wars. For his efforts in WWI, Griffith received the Silver Star, the Purple Heart, Legion of Honor and the Croix de Guerre as well as four battle clasps. He was wounded so severely during the First World War that word was sent home that he had been killed. A French surgeon operated on Griffith right on the battlefield without any anesthetic, saving his life. Griffith served as a major and a lieutenant colonel, becoming a colonel in January of 1944. He was also appointed chief of the Veteran Personnel Division of the Selective Service System. A parade and other events were held on Paul H. Griffith Homecoming Day in Uniontown on November 16, 1946. (Walter "Buzz" Storey collection.)

Chapter 3
Delightful Pastimes

Armand Leonelli, father-in-law of the author, once was employed at the Manos. He is shown here walking in front of the Thrift Drug Store on his way from the theater. (Author's collection.)

The ultra-modern Manos Theater opened August 20, 1941 with a showing of *The Hamilton Woman* starring Vivian Leigh and Lawrence Olivier. The theater was built by veteran Greensburg showman Michael Manos who came to this country from Athens, Greece in 1901 with the equivalent of two dollars of American currency in his pocket. The Manos installed a Western Electric Microphonic sound system for the perfect reproduction of sound pictures, two thousand comfortable seats with ribbed mohair backs and one of the finest lobbies in this part of the state. Manos architect Victor A. Rigaumont had previously designed over 150 theaters. (Uniontown Public Library collection.)

One of the most elaborate showplaces in Pennsylvania was the State Theater designed by architect Thomas Lamb in 1922. A mural depicting the allegorical figures of music, drama and art was painted on the arch over the stage. A $40,000 Pleubet Master Organ in the pit provided accompaniment for the silent movies. Four boxes graced each side of the theater until the introduction of wide-screen movies. The State also hosted some of the country's greatest big band performers: Paul Whiteman, Glen Gray and the Dorsey Brothers. In recent years the Grand Old Lady of Main Street has been restored to her former splendor. (Rev. Peter Malik collection, right. Katie Sepkovic, left collection.)

Jack Chidester takes time out to cool off with a twenty-five cent bottle of R.C. Cola at the 1954-55 Billiards Tournament held at the State Pool Hall while "Moonie" takes a shot at the corner pocket. Rudy Hlastala of Pittsburgh Road, North Union Township, won the competition that season. The referees were under pressure with so many highly skilled players in this male-dominated sport. (Dale "Chilly" Williams collection.)

Louis Chaconas managed the State Billiards Parlor from 1953 to 1978. Prior to Chaconas, Clarence Davis and George Hardy managed the pool hall. Chaconas closed the establishment due to a technicality and standards in running that type of business. (Dale "Chilly" Williams collection.)

It was "standing room only" when 14-times world champion billiard player Willie Mosconi and the guys got together to shoot pool at the State Billiards Parlor at 33 East Main Street. Born in Philadelphia in 1913, Mosconi was a child prodigy who began competing around 1931. His first championship was in 1941 and, except for 1943 and 1949, he defended his title every year until 1955. In the mid 1950s he gave exhibitions throughout the country to help promote the sport of billiards. (Dale "Chilly" Williams collection.)

In 1907 Charles Gorley began damming up a crystal clear mountain stream located on his property. Brothers Clarence and Wilmer Wilkey were hired to build a dam for the mile-long lake that took almost three years to complete. Knowing the popularity of his lake for boating, fishing and swimming, Gorley began work on a fabulous mountain hotel in 1921. The grand opening was on July 17, 1923. Hundreds of people attended parties, conventions, reunions and business meetings at Gorley's Hotel. Talented local bands played swing music on the weekends in the classy El Patio nightclub at the hotel. (Uniontown Public Library collection.)

George Silver, seen here as a shadowy silhouette, was a well-liked dance orchestra leader and master of ceremonies twice nominated for the office of Uniontown mayor. He frequently traveled to New York City with a group of local musicians and it was there that he acquired the name Club Kentucky for his orchestra. Silver, who trained at Ohio's Dana Music Institute, served as the president of the Musicians Society and was also associated with his family's business, the Silvers' Music Mart. (*News Standard*.)

An extremely talented local musician, John Vaselenak kept the Big Band sound going in Fayette County from the 1930s into the 1990s. His Johnny Vass Orchestra played regularly at the Lucky Star Inn in Hopwood and also appeared at the Sunset Ballroom on Route 40 and at the former St. James Country Club, now known as Linden Hall. Vaselenak was hired to play at Cuppies in Malden by the owner Syl Colletti who was a close friend to Dean Martin. John Vaselenak remembered hearing Dean Martin sing in Fairbank at a place called Dooley's. Angelo Quarzo, who signed on big bands like Gene Krupa and Sammy Kaye, also hired the Johnny Vass Orchestra. The first two bands to be broadcast over WMBS radio in Uniontown were George Silvers' and Johnny Vass's. (Johnny Vass collection.)

Ten thousand people from all over the county enjoyed Uniontown's great Centennial celebration on Saturday July 4,1896. The 12-mile bicycle race along the National Road from Fayette Street to the Village of Searights proved to be an exciting event. There were thirty-two entries. A. E. Neff of Irwin, who came in second in the race, is shown here pedaling along the course. (The Haky family collection.)

Rutter's Band, organized in 1856 by George W. Rutter, was the official band of the Tenth Regiment and provided the music at Uniontown's Centennial celebration. George's son, ex-Burgess Frank Rutter was once the leader of this band. (Uniontown Public Library collection.)

Some fans are shown with the famous McCormick Amateurs baseball team and Rutter's Band in front of the Exchange in Franklin, PA in 1896. The Amateurs were rated one of the standout teams in the eastern section of the country back in the 1890s. William C. McCormick, shown in the center front, managed the baseball team. Some of the original players on the team were second baseman Smith "Stump" Whaley; Charles 'Red' Wilhelm, infielder; shortstop John Buttermore; Charles Smith, utility; Frank

Hagan, third baseman; Billy McCormick, manager; catcher Bruce F. Sterling; Alph "Sharkey" Beall, first baseman; pitcher Owen "Jake" Altman; Harry Wilhelm, pitcher and right fielder; William Lemon, pitcher and middle fielder. (Uniontown Public Library collection.)

Entertainment abounded. A baseball game was played at Continental No. 1. There was an aviation show by Charles H. Walsh of the Curtiss Company. A band performed in concert. The county fire departments demonstrated their skills. Prizes were awarded for the best-decorated automobiles at the auto show parade. A high wire act appeared at the First National Bank building. This little girl is walking to the courthouse lawn to see the Punch and Judy show. James G. Johnston, the oldest living former burgess of Uniontown, presented an historical speech. The grand finale was a fireworks display set off at the Semans' property on West Berkeley Street. (Uniontown Public Library collection.)

Uniontown's Old Home Week celebration was held August 26-31, 1912. Public buildings and homes were spruced up with patriotic bunting. Prizes were awarded for the property that was most improved and best decorated for the occasion. (Uniontown Public Library collection.)

Do You Remember When...

Playing marbles has been a popular game with children for centuries. These young boys are showing off their skill in an early 1900s competition. (Author's collection.)

Little Harriet "Hattie" Mabel Blacka poses with her doll baby and the family dog at the Blacka homestead in Dunbar. Hattie was born June 3, 1906, the daughter of Albert and Blanche Blacka. Hattie's daughter, Betty Wilson remembers two dolls in the house when she grew up there. "One was Mom's and the other was her younger sister Polly's," she recalled. (Betty O. Wilson collection.)

This young lad had his photograph taken at the T.A. Sharpnack Photography Studio in Brownsville around 1900. He brought along his favorite game, the stick and wooden hoop. The child would try to keep the hoop in a standing position by rolling it with the stick while running alongside. Children have played this game for centuries. (John Carom collection.)

Do You Remember When...

Hundreds of spectators lined Route 119 North to watch the Soap Box Derby held in July 1954. Thirteen-year-old Francis Takoch, sponsored by Fayette Welding Company, won first place and the right to race at the All American Soap Box Derby in Akron, Ohio. Runner-up was Keith Vail sponsored by the Union Supply Company. General Motors, United War Veteran's Association of Uniontown, Chick Lee Chevrolet Company and Uniontown Newspapers, Inc. sponsored Fayette County's second annual post-war derby. (Uniontown Public Library collection)

These children are enjoying freshly pressed apple cider on the Charles Gates property near Fairchance in 1910. They will take home their crocks and buckets filled with this delicious drink. The children may have been from the Gates and Derry families. (William G. Brown collection.)

Dunbar Township High School produced some powerhouse athletes, both male and female. Their school newspaper, *The Sentinel*, recorded German, Perryopolis, West Newton, Scottdale, Jeannette, Connellsville, Uniontown and South Brownsville high school teams as some of Dunbar's rivals. These team photographs were taken in Dunbar in 1916. (Author's collection.)

In 1903 Harry Beeson built the West End Theater on the former site of General George C. Marshall's boyhood home. The first show was the *Sultan of Sulu*, a production from New York. Live plays, silent movies, burlesque shows, sporting events and political functions were held in the theater. Beeson setup a bookstore in one of the rooms. In 1947 the Veterans of Foreign Wars acquired and redesigned the building. (Haky family collection.)

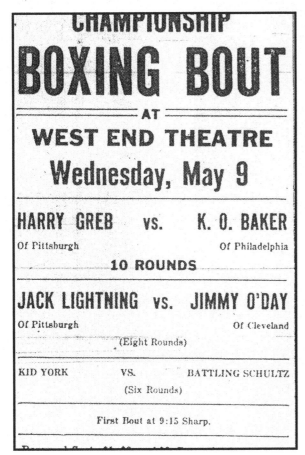

Boxer Harry Greb was one of the greatest boxers of all times and the only opponent to beat world heavyweight champion Gene Tunney. Greb had over 100 fights before he won the light heavyweight title and then later the middleweight crown. "The Human Windmill" was born in Pittsburgh, June 6, 1894 and began boxing in 1913. Hundreds of Fayette County boxing fans came out to witness him box at the West End Theater on May 9, 1917. Harry Greb liked Uniontown's atmosphere and Gorley's Lake Hotel so much that he had his manager set up a training camp at Gorley's for ten days. (*News Standard*, bottom. Author's collection, top right.)

The Titlow Hotel was one of the finest and most desirable hostelries in the county. This centrally located hotel with an electric passenger elevator and fifty sleeping rooms had easy access to the train depot. An interurban trolley system once passed directly in front of its spacious steel veranda. The bar was stocked with the finest foreign and domestic wines and liquors and the food was superb. Proprietor and operator George Titlow was known as a sincere, accommodating and gracious host. (*Evening Genius Illustrated Industrial Edition.*)

Robert Rohm Wooddy enjoyed bartending at the Titlow Hotel. He earned notoriety as the oldest active bartender in Uniontown. Wooddy once worked as a fire boss for the W. J. Rainey Coal and Coke Co. at the Revere and Clyde mines and was a member of the local police force from 1918-23. (Patricia Dailey collection.)

Maud Powell, shown here in 1908, was one of the most accomplished violinists in the world during the early 1900s. Known to many Americans for her musical skills, she was a women's rights activist as well. Prior to a sold-out performance at Uniontown's West End Theater on January 7, 1920, Ms. Powell became ill and Dr. A. E. Crow was called to her room at the Titlow Hotel where she passed away the following day. Though relatively unknown to the average person today, Powell is revered among violinists worldwide. (Author's collection)

The Penn Theater on East Main Street was a favorite Saturday afternoon destination for young boys who enjoyed cowboy movies. When it opened on November 16, 1914 every seat was reserved for the first feature shown - an Italian motion picture. The theater was operated for years by the Penn State Amusement Company that was later acquired by the Manos Company. The Penn Theater closed about 1952 to make way for the expansion of G. C. Murphy Company's 5 & 10 ¢ Store. (Author's collection.)

The Opera House at the corner of Pittsburgh and Peter Streets in Uniontown held its grand opening on April 30, 1883 with the famous actor Joseph Johnson playing the role of Rip Van Winkle. The Opera House was built in the Renaissance Revival style with a Second Empire style roof. Years later a bank was built next to it that overshadowed the fine old-time theater. The building is now home to the Masonic Lodge #1. (David Priest and the Masons Lodge.)

Al G. Field, born Alfred G. Hatfield and reared in Brownsville, is shown here in 1912 with his two friends Court and Scott. Field was thought to be one of the best entertainers in the United States. He was a circus clown, an author and manager of a traveling minstrel show. Locally, he handled performances by the Hostetler Blind Family. (from *Watch Yourself Go By* by Al G. Field.)

Mr. and Mrs. Frank Semans enjoyed a beautiful mansion, exotic Japanese Gardens, a pond and boathouse on their Mont View Street property in Uniontown. They were very generous to the less fortunate and would invite young people from the community to the estate for a day of fun. Many beautiful homes now grace their former property and the remainder of the Japanese Gardens is privately owned. (Uniontown Public Library collection.)

Do You Remember When...

During the warm summer months Joseph Sante of Phillips enjoyed fishing at Indian Head. Many rivers and streams in Fayette County can be a wonderful place to relax and enjoy but when the water levels are high and the currents are swift, they can also be dangerous. In 1941, Joseph's two daughters, Constance, 9, and Josephine, 2, slipped and fell into the reservoir. Joseph drowned when he made a heroic but unsuccessful attempt to rescue them. Other family members saved the girls. Joseph was the author's grandfather. (Connie Sante Dutko collection.)

A few old photographs and postcards have emerged showing the waterfall and huge boulders on Bear Run before Fallingwater was built. Around 1890 a Masonic organization used the property as a vacation club. The Kaufmann Department Store owners used the property in 1916 as a vacation camp for their employees. Around 1921 the Kaufmann family built a small mountain cottage at Bear Run. In 1933 the Kaufmanns bought the property as their personal mountain retreat. Frank Lloyd Wright built Fallingwater for the Kaufmanns in 1936. (Clinton Piper and the Western Pennsylvania Conservancy)

Johnny Weissmuller, a.k.a. Tarzan of Hollywood fame, visited his friend Paul Wyatt in Brownsville several times. Both Weissmuller and Wyatt won Olympic medals in 1924 and 1928 for swimming. It is said that the pair being in perfect physical condition once dove off the Tri-County Bridge in Brownsville. Both also had ties to southwestern Pennsylvania. Wyatt was born in the historic Peter Colley Tavern in Brier Hill. His friend Weissmuller spent his early years in Windber near Johnstown. (Charles Rohrer collection.)

Do You Remember When...

Connellsville native John Woodruff brought fame
to Fayette County when he won a gold medal in the
Berlin Olympics in 1936. Woodruff, a student at the
University of Pittsburgh, took the 300-meter event
before 20,000 spectators in Colombes Stadium. He
was awarded the key to the City of Connellsville for
his great achievements. (Connellsville High School
yearbook.)

Civic-minded J. V.
Thompson hosted many
Fayette County Inter-High
School Track and Field
Meets at his lovely Oak
Hill Estate. At the first meet
on May 13, 1916, over
one thousand spectators
cheered on their favorite
athletes from Uniontown,
Connellsville, Dunbar,
Fayette City, North Union,
McClellandtown, Point
Marion, South Brownsville
and other schools. (Becky
Wilhelm McGarvey
collection.)

Skilled racecar drivers from far and wide raced their speed demons on the board track at the Uniontown Speedway east of Uniontown. Bets were made on favorites and the winners went home with hefty cash prizes and shiny trophies. (Becky Wilhelm McGarvey collection, right. Joanne Politano collection, bottom.)

An early Packard automobile was on display at the National Auto Garage on West Fayette Street during Auto Week in Uniontown. The Dodge Brothers were offering touring cars or roadsters for just $785. Hundreds of dollars were spent throughout the county to convert local garages into fitting display rooms for the sleek shining pleasure cars and powerful commercial models. (Uniontown Public Library collection.)

These two motorcyclists are pulled over on the side of the road near the Water Street Garage in Brownsville. The man on the left has a Harley while the one on the right has an Indian cycle. Motorcycle racing was a popular sport in Fayette County. (Author's collection.)

In the 1950s, Rainbow Park boasted one of the largest swimming pools in this area as well as an amusement park-type swing, a huge sandbox, a skating rink, a dance hall and covered pavilions for reunions and picnics. This Fairchance area park, located in Haydentown at the foot of Mud Pike, also had an 18-hole miniature golf course. Several streetcars added a nostalgic touch to the picturesque setting. Visitors from all over Fayette County delighted in the many diversions offered at Rainbow Park during the summer months. (Rita Foriska Miller collection.)

Shady Grove Park in Lemont Furnace was the equivalent of Kennywood Park to those of us who spent our summers there. During the early years, visitors to Shady Grove enjoyed paddling their canoes on the pond, swimming in the warm water or sun bathing on the beach. The wooden pavilion towering above the park was the scene of many family reunions and had ideal acoustics for dances. There was a concession stand, shooting gallery, merry-go-round, roller coaster and numerous games. Famous Big Band leaders Jimmy Dorsey and Guy Lombardo performed at Shady Grove. Around 1930 a gigantic oval cement swimming pool with diving boards and a fountain were added to the park. The powder-blue pool with both shallow and deep crystal clear water continued to be the main attraction at this special Fayette County hot spot for years. Both the Cabot and Tesauro families have been owners of Shady Grove. (Uniontown Public Library collection.)

Do You Remember When...

The Stone House along Route 40 East has seen many owners come and go throughout its lifetime but its facade has remained almost unchanged. Uniontown businessman George Titlow was one of the previous owners. Well-known politician and prominent Fayette County resident Andrew Stewart opened it as the Fayette Springs Hotel in 1822 for those taking the long hard journey over the National Road. Stewart owned over 80,000 acres of prime real estate and the township was named for him. (Uniontown Public Library collection.)

John Kennedy Lacock guided an excursion of prominent men including several history professors intent on retracing Braddock's Road. In this rare candid photograph, Lacock and his associates are seen resting in the mountains with James Hadden who is sporting a black derby and a long white beard. Hadden was usually behind the camera photographing others. (Uniontown Public Library collection.)

Fayette County has the perfect geological conditions for the existence of deep caves. It is rumored that outlaws hid gold and other treasures in several caves throughout the county. The caves in Fayette County's mountain area have always been a main attraction. These people are relaxing at the mouth of a cave near the Summit Mountain. Look closely and you will see that their shotguns are near-at-hand just in case they encounter some wildlife, or even worse, one of the notorious Fayette County gangs. (Uniontown Public Library collection.)

Hillcrest Roller Rink was a popular entertainment spot for skating and dancing in the Connellsville area. Manager Thomas F. Means helped maintain the building and planned fun-filled activities for the patrons. A fire destroyed the Hillcrest, its furnishings, the PA system, roller skates and two automobiles. The new rink and building were about a year old when this photograph was taken. (William G. Brown collection.)

Two long gone eras of Hopwood's history are blended together in this photograph. In 1818 William Morris built the Morris Tavern, a stone house along the National Road. After Morris retired, it was referred to as the German D. Hair Tavern. The tavern was converted in 1939 into the Majorette, a popular diner and dairy bar. Peppy carhops dressed in white tasseled boots, round skirts and hats adorned with ostrich feathers delivered modern fast food to customers seated in their automobiles. (The Fayette County Historical Society collection.)

Although ice skating had been popular for many decades the North Pole Ice Skating Rink was the first modern rink of its kind in the city. The Alexander family opened the rink in 1960 and operated it for the next ten years. Children and adults from all parts of the county enjoyed drinking delicious hot chocolate from the concession stand and warming themselves in front of the cozy fireplace. The same ice-making equipment used to freeze the rink in the winter was used to make ice to sell in the summer when it was moved so that Saturday night sock hops could be accommodated with Leon Sykes as the disc jockey. (Joseph C. Alexander, Jr. and Adele Alexander Congelio collection.)

Little Emily Newcomer is sitting on a pony near Santa's workshop. Emily has just whispered her wish list to Santa Claus. The Lynch Store was among those that set up a place where children could talk to Old Saint Nick. Hard candies, nuts and fruit were given to the little boys and girls. Clothing styles have changed over the years and Santa's costume is no exception. (Author's collection.)

The Soldiers' Orphan School was once located on the site of Dunbar's Camp in Jumonville. The children who lived at this temporary mountain home were well cared for during their stay. These children are taking advantage of a recent snowfall to build a snowman and dress him with a cap from one child's uniform. (Uniontown Public Library collection)

Oak Hill estate was illuminated with candles burning in carved jack-o'-lanterns every Halloween eve as J. V. and Hunnie Hawes Thompson's guests gathered for an annual masquerade party. The gracious host and hostess served expensive delicacies, desserts and drinks at their huge mansion. (Uniontown Public Library collection.)

The State Billiards Parlor hosted bowling tournaments in the lower level of the building. These dapper looking gentlemen are part of the Richmond Radiator Duckpin Bowling Team. Bowling enthusiasts from all over Fayette County came here to participate in or observe the competitions. (Dale "Chilly" Williams collection.)

Bowling leagues throughout the area were extremely competitive. Companies would sponsor their employee teams. This team was named for the Eastern Freight Line, Inc., located on Gallatin Avenue in North Union Township. Paul Glover was the company's president. Although the bowlers pictured here have not been identified, some of the Eastern Freight Line team were Bill Yantko, Tye Rafitz, Don Jenny, Emil Ciarrocchi, Jack Jones, Alice Blazek, Johnnie Blazek, Elizabeth Moleck, Lefty Tomko, Charlie Show, Helen Pratt, Walt Lion, Al Carolla, Betty Frazee and Wayne Pratt. (Author's collection.)

Do You Remember When...

Did you know that a Uniontown man named the Pittsburgh Steelers? On January 2, 1940 Arnold Goldberg, sports editor of the Daily News Standard, entered a contest for the purpose of renaming the professional Pittsburgh Football Club. Arthur J. Rooney, the president of the club, informed Mr. Goldberg that his entry had been selected out of thousands received. Mr. Goldberg won season tickets to the football games to be played at Forbes Field. (Uniontown Public Library collection.)

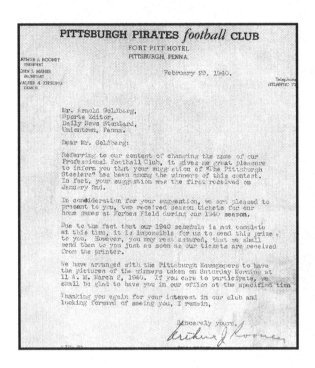

The Uniontown Red Raider Basketball Champions of 1964 are featured in a parade passing in front of Park and Lafayette Schools across from the Red and White Supermarket on Connellsville Street. Coach A. J. Everhart, Jr. is riding in the front of a Uniontown fire truck while some of his talented players, Paul Yezbak, Ray Parson, Patrick "Doc" Yates, John Miller, Jim Rae, Chuckie Beckwith and Ray Stevens wave to their fans. Everhart's undefeated team was considered to be one of the highest-ranking in Pennsylvania's high school basketball history and some players went onto professional status. (Carol Dutko Marshaus collection.)

John Lujack, number "25" in this photograph, was a great all-around athlete who earned national respect in the sport of football. This 1942 graduate of Connellsville High School believed that most of his success started during his years playing sports in his hometown. In 1946 and 1947 Lujack played in back-to-back national championships for Notre Dame, winning the Heisman Trophy in 1947. He went on to play for the Chicago Bears. Lujack was an All-NFL quarterback in 1950 and was later elected to the National Football Foundation Hall of Fame. (The Coker, 1941.)

A. Patrick Pallini spent much of his childhood at Oak Hill, the home of coal baron J. V. Thompson. He and J. V.'s grand-daughter, Evelyn Thompson were once caught riding their ponies through the reception hall of the mansion. Pat's parents were Pasquale and Angelica, the butler and cook and trusted friends of Thompson. Pallini became an experienced jockey. In 1933 he and this running horse, Frizzle won two races during the same day at South Park in Pittsburgh. (A. Patrick Pallini collection.)

The 16th annual Great Dawson Fair took place between September 16 and 19, 1930 with Mrs. H. T. Cochran as acting president. Three daredevil teams entered the half-mile bareback Roman standing horse race presented by Lt. Scava's Gendarmes. Some of the horses actually leaped over another horse and a human hurdle. There wasn't a seat available in the stands for the two-horse chariot races. Fairgoers could also enjoy displays of textiles and lace, tasty preserves and canned fruits or view waterfowl, turkeys, sheep, swine, horses, rabbits and cattle. The events were topped off with a band concert and Dawson Fair's famous fireworks display. (Dawson Fair booklet.)

W. Brown, Sr., Hagan Gates, Katherine Gates, Ms. Brown, Jenn Sutton and G. Sutton are standing in front of one of the Dawson Fair picnic pavilions. (William G. Brown collection.)

Do You Remember When...

Chapter 4
Booming Businesses

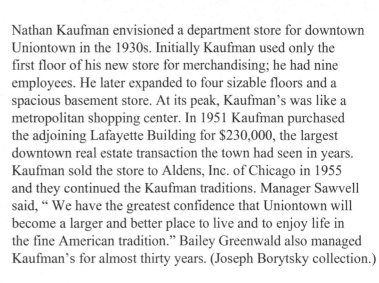

Nathan Kaufman envisioned a department store for downtown Uniontown in the 1930s. Initially Kaufman used only the first floor of his new store for merchandising; he had nine employees. He later expanded to four sizable floors and a spacious basement store. At its peak, Kaufman's was like a metropolitan shopping center. In 1951 Kaufman purchased the adjoining Lafayette Building for $230,000, the largest downtown real estate transaction the town had seen in years. Kaufman sold the store to Aldens, Inc. of Chicago in 1955 and they continued the Kaufman traditions. Manager Sawvell said, " We have the greatest confidence that Uniontown will become a larger and better place to live and to enjoy life in the fine American tradition." Bailey Greenwald also managed Kaufman's for almost thirty years. (Joseph Borytsky collection.)

Many Fayette County buildings have been erected over underground mines. For a long time this house fascinated those passing by it on Route 119 in Connellsville. Mine subsidence caused the home to tilt farther each year until it finally collapsed. (Uniontown Public Library collection.)

In order to satisfy the company quota, miners had to dig and lift heavy loads of coal by hand day in and day out. Ventilation was almost nonexistent and some mines were extremely dry, generating excessive rock and coal dust, harmful to the workers. Miners were susceptible to tuberculosis. American miners between the ages of fifteen and twenty-four had twice the death rate of workers of the same age in other occupations. The foundation was being laid for miner's asthma or black lung claims. (Author's collection.)

Outcroppings of bituminous coal can often be found close to the surface throughout Fayette County. Some landowners mined what were referred to as "country banks", "gopher holes" or "father and son" mines on their property. (Author's collection.)

About one mile south of Perryopolis lays Star Junction, a flourishing coal-mining town during the early 1900s. The coke ovens went into operation there around 1893. This patch town was owned by the Washington Coal and Coke Company founded by James Cochran of Dawson. Production declined in the 1920s and 30s and ceased in the 1950s. (Author's collection.)

Men and mules were the backbone of the coal and coke industry during the early days. This team is standing in front of a wooden coal tipple at a slope mine near the foot of the Laurel Mountains close to Fairchance. The barefooted child riding on the mule may be part of the work crew. (William G. Brown collection.)

The first coke works in Trotter, Dunbar Township, were owned and operated by the Connellsville Gas-Coal Company. Their property consisted of 3100 acres, one thousand acres of which was leased to the Cambria Iron Company. In 1864 the company's assets were $500,000. The coal vein at Trotter averaged nine feet deep. The coal was higher in fixed carbon and coke yield and lower in sulfur content and ash than most other coal, proving the theory that the Connellsville coking coal is superior. Trotter was near New Haven Junction, a little more than

a mile out of the Opossum Run Branch of the Pennsylvania Railroad. The village of Trotter was named for Charles W. Trotter. (Dunbar Township yearbook.)

Do You Remember When...

Around 1900 the Hagan Ice Cream Company hauled 100 gallons of ice cream from Uniontown into Masontown by horse and buggy for the Honsaker reunion. Making and delivering this much of the frozen treat during the early days was no small job, and the accomplishment did boost the business's reputation in the area. (Hagan Anniversary.)

Later Hagan's would have delicatessen/ice cream stores in Uniontown and Hopwood. (Hagan Anniversary.)

At one time the National Biscuit Company, aka Nabisco, delivered their delicious snacks by horse and wagon to the local grocery stores. The Pittsburgh-based company grew in size and transported crackers and cookies into Fayette and the surrounding counties. They introduced the community to mass-produced sanitized packaging. Oreo cookies, first introduced in 1912, and Ritz crackers both quickly became best sellers. Children enjoyed the delicious taste of Nabisco's Barnum Animal Crackers and delighted in decorating their Christmas trees with the empty boxes that were designed like circus cages. Nabisco had a major branch and warehouse in Uniontown at 58-62 Dunbar Street. (Author's collection.)

Do You Remember When...

Coca Cola Bottling was once owned and managed by Earl E. Keller and his sons. The company was started as Keller's Soda Water Works on South Street next to King's Feed Store on November 11, 1911 by Harry Keller, who came to Uniontown as a member of the Uniontown baseball team of the old P.O.M. League. The business later moved to the rear of 45 Pittsburgh Street. When Earl's brother, Harry Keller joined the business in 1916, they operated as Keller Bros. Quality Beverages. The Kellers began their association with Coca Cola in 1919. Their facility bottled both Coca Cola in regular and king-size bottles and Blue Ridge Quality Beverages. The business was incorporated May 1, 1937. The new Art Deco-styled home of Coca Cola at 244 Pittsburgh Street in North Union Township was first opened to the public in October of 1941. The facility provided complete convenience for the employees as well as customers who loved to sip on this cool, dark fizzy drink. (Tom Merryman collection.)

Fayette Brewing Company was incorporated on August 25, 1900 and employed 25 men. The company owned ten wagons and twenty-five horses. They brewed two brands of beer: Standard, sold in kegs, and Lafayette Export, for bottling. Their brew was superior because they used the best barley and hops that money could buy. The aging process took place in cold storage rooms for months. Fayette Brewing's quality beer sold at the same price as other beers that were brewed for half the cost. The company could produce up to 200 cases of beer per day. (Uniontown Public Library collection.)

The North Pole Ice Company was founded by Liberato "Lee" Alexander (center) and Dan Angelo Izzi (back). The company opened on July 4, 1929 and on that day ice was offered to customers at no charge. Many customers had block ice delivered to their homes daily to cool their wooden iceboxes and to preserve perishable food items. Block ice was sold at that time for one penny a pound. The railroads were also a major consumer of ice. The iceman would pull blocks of ice up from the truck to the top hatches of the train cars with ropes and ice tongs. The four hatches on the boxcars had to be filled to keep perishable items cold in transit. (Joseph C. Alexander, Jr. and Adele Alexander Congelio collection.)

Do You Remember When...

Yee Sing operated the Star Laundry at 61 Morgantown Street, Uniontown. Similar businesses were often called "Chinese laundries." Sing employed three people when he opened on April 1, 1901. The Star Laundry was one of the best in the county, equipped with the finest machinery available and employing hard working men and women. Yee Sing's brothers operated laundries in California, Brownsville and Greensburg. (*Evening Genius Illustrated Industrial Edition.*)

Richard "Dickey" Richardson was a familiar sight around Fayette County making deliveries in his horse-drawn wagon. Born into slavery around 1800 in Virginia, Mr. Richardson received his emancipation papers in 1843. Before the Civil War he came to Pennsylvania and lived at Addison, Somerset County. Richardson buried some valuables near the tollhouse in Addison, but when he returned for his treasures he was unable to find them. Despite this loss, he went on to own several properties and to become a prosperous citizen. Richardson once resided at the McCormick addition of Uniontown. He told acquaintances that he was at least 100 years old. "Dickey" Richardson passed away in 1899 and was buried beside his wife and child in the old Presbyterian Cemetery. (Walter "Buzz" Storey collection.)

Beekeeper Charles Gates of Haydentown never wore gloves or the customary veil when tending his colony of bees. Well-known throughout the Fairchance area, Gates supplied many of his friends and neighbors with the purest honey. At one time Pennsylvania produced about five million pounds of honey each year. (William G. Brown collection.)

Michael's Infant and Children's Shop became a shopping tradition for generations of parents. Businesswoman Flora Fell Michael, wife of J.J. Michael, operated the family business and specialty store at 55 South Gallatin Avenue in Uniontown. A man is standing near an impressive late model sedan parked in front of the store. (Sol Michael collection.)

Sebastian Spering Kresge was the founder of the S.S. Kresge Company, now known as Kmart Corporation. S.S. Kresge's 5 & 10 ¢ store in Uniontown was at 16 East Main Street during the 1930s. Merchandise was sold here at bargain prices. Shoppers could enjoy a cherry coke at the lunch counter while deciding whether to order the blue plate special. (*News Standard*, 1933.)

The sales and display room of the Frederick Music Store was located at 49 West Main Street. It was owned by businessman W.F. Frederick, one of Uniontown's millionaires, who was engaged in enterprises throughout Uniontown, Pittsburgh and the tri-state area. The music store carried Philco and Zenith radios, band instruments, pianos and even electric refrigerators. (*News Standard*, 1933)

Richmond Radiator Company manufactured radiators and boilers at their plant north of Uniontown and was the largest employer in the area. Richmond Radiator's forerunner was the Richmond Stove Company at Norwich, Connecticut, founded in 1867 by Apollo Richmond. Around 1899 the company became associated with L.G. McCrum and George B. Howell, the operators of the Uniontown Acme Radiator Company. The McCrum-Howell Company operated successfully for a number of years but fell into decline around 1912, resulting in involuntary bankruptcy. They reorganized and continued business as the Richmond Radiator Company. (Uniontown booklet.)

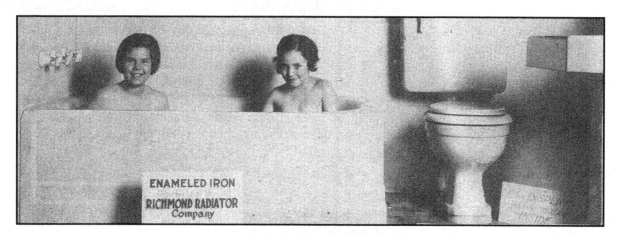

Uniontown Hardware and Supply Company was one of the Fayette County businesses that carried choice bath fixtures made by the Richmond Radiator Company and Enamel Plant. Ann and Martha selected the custom-colored orchid bathtub for their parent's home during the 1930s. (*News Standard*, 1933, middle.)

Do You Remember When...

Anyone who resided in Fayette County during the 1950s and 60s will remember the W. T. Grant store. It had varnished wooden flooring, sincere and confidant salespersons and, most of all, great hot dogs and sodas! Grant's was founded in 1928 and expanded to over 500 stores from coast to coast. The Grant's in Uniontown grew to double the size of the original store. (*Herald Standard*.)

The Berkowitz family operated several businesses in Fayette County. Michael Berkowitz started a shirt factory in South Union that bore his name. During the early 1900s, Jacob Berkowitz operated a dry cleaning business at 19 Morgantown Street in Uniontown. This photograph shows Mr. Berkowitz with other employees and managers in the office of an unnamed knitting mill in Pennsylvania. (Author's collection.)

The long-established Ross Brothers Sporting Store on South Street was originally at 54 West Peter Street. In this 1933 photograph, Louis, Tommy, Al and Winfield pose with some of their favorite sporting equipment. Notice the knickers that the young men are wearing. Albert A. Ross was the owner and manager of his family's business at the time this photograph was taken. (*News Standard*, 1933.)

Anchor Hocking Corporation moved from Long Island, New York to Connellsville in 1941 and twenty-five new homes were to be built for the key families involved in the transfer. The plastic department began operations in May. Over four hundred employees worked here and at one time the annual payroll was approximately $2,000,000. (Author's collection.)

The Houze Convex Glass Company was a major industry in Point Marion and the county, famous for producing novelties, trays, lamps and fine glassware. The famous Houze family of Belgium started the business. Five hundred people once worked at the glass factory. The employed were craftsmen in their own right; veteran glassblowers worked alongside specialists in other techniques such as pressing colored glass for trays and ornaments. (*News Standard*, 1933.)

The Thompson Glass Company produced high quality pieces of pressed glassware at their facilities on South Mount Vernon Avenue in South Union Township. The discovery of natural gas near Uniontown had attracted the attention of the glass industry, and some "practical glass men" from Pittsburgh organized the business named in honor of Jasper M. Thompson, the father of coal baron J. V. Thompson. In the 1880s the company produced goblets, pitchers, compotes, bowls and oil lamps in such exquisite patterns as Torpedo or Pygmy, Bow Tie, Summit, Tile and Thompson 77. Collectors and dealers seek out these lovely pieces of glassware that were once a part of the dining

services and lighting of many Victorian era households in the area. The pressed glassware was manufactured during a limited time period due to a gas shortage. (Donated to the Uniontown Public Library collection by Ed and Sally Reed, Uniontown Glass historians.)

At Uniontown's centennial celebration, July 4, 1896, two thousand coal and coke workers marched in a parade that showcased a float with a handmade model coal mine from 1796 and a new-fashioned model of the Leisenring No. 2 mine, 1896. (Haky family collection.)

Mules were used in the coal mines and were bred for their power and efficiency. When the mines were very deep, mules were preferred to horses because they could pull a heavier load, they were more sure-footed in the dark and a mule could be shod for half the cost of shoeing a horse. Most of the mules were very dark brown or black. White mules were banned because miners thought they looked ghostly and could frighten mules and miners alike. (Author's collection.)

The Everson Car and Repair Shops were constructed in 1895 on Pennsylvania Avenue in Everson by the H. C. Frick Coke Company for fabricating and repairing the mining cars that hauled coal and coke. The shops were ideally located between the Frick coal lands in Fayette and Westmoreland counties. This photograph, taken during the fall of 1907, shows Emmanuel C. Malik, Sr. standing in the back row, fourth from the left, behind his boss who is dressed in a suit and wearing a bowler hat. One of Malik's sons, Andrew Malik, is leaning in the doorway. (Rev. Peter Malik collection.)

Do You Remember When...

Orville Eberly will be remembered for his keen sense of business and commerce as well as his philanthropy and community service. He was married to Ruth Moore Eberly and was the father of Robert E. Eberly, Mrs. Margaret E. George and Mrs. Carolyn E. Blaney. Eberly, who established the Eberly Coal and Coke Co. in Uniontown, began working in the coal mines as an electrician, attended night school and received his fire boss and mine foreman certificates. Later he and

William E. Snee became business associates, resulting in the exploration and development of Summit Gas Field near Uniontown and the Accident Field in Maryland. Orville Eberly was instrumental in bringing a campus of Pennsylvania State University to our county. He established the Eberly Foundation that provided hundreds of scholarships to Fayette County students. Eberly served as the President of the Board of Trustees of the Uniontown Hospital. He was a major shareholder and board chairman of the former Gallatin Bank. The entire Eberly family and associates of the Eberly Family Foundation have always been dedicated to the improvement of schools, libraries, charities and the arts, as well as the economical advancement of our community. (Uniontown Public Library collection.)

The Uniontown Hospital received a $3.5 million dollar expansion in 1965. The new seven-story addition adjoined the wing that was added in 1957. It was built in an "L" shape at the northeast corner of the present structure on Berkeley Street, between Delaware Avenue and McClellandtown Road. The Uniontown Hospital continues to be one of Fayette County's largest employers. This unique bird's eye view also shows part of the School of Nursing, Oak Grove Cemetery and Route 40. The Uniontown Hospital's School of Nursing began in 1904, graduating a class of four nurses in 1907. The School of Nursing building seen here was erected in 1948. (Uniontown Public Library collection.)

Do You Remember When...

Josiah VanKirk Thompson was best known as a banker and coal land broker, but he was also one of the most respected and well-liked businessmen in southwestern Pennsylvania. His life was like a modern-day soap opera. At one time he reigned as a coal baron, living in a mansion filled with treasures from all over the world. Thompson built an eleven-story skyscraper in Uniontown that is still one of the tallest buildings in this part of the country. (Uniontown Public Library collection.)

Shrewd Fayette County businessman James I. Feathers and Senator William E. Crow attended the liquidation sale of J.V. Thompson's bank building on February 23, 1918 with thousands of dollars of cash in hand. W.A. Stone made the first bid of a half-million dollars. Feathers and Stone were bidding so furiously that other bidders quickly dropped out. Stone threw in a $691,000 bid, but J. I. wasn't easily intimidated. He raised his hand and shouted, "$700,000." "I'm done," said Stone. Auctioneer Fee cried out Feathers' bid for a third time. James I. Feathers got a "two for one" that day by winning both the First National Bank Building and the Grand Opera Building. The skyscraper can be seen in the background of the below left photo. Feathers' home at the corner of Fayette and Mill Streets has been torn down.(Uniontown Public Library collection, left. Rev. Peter Malik collection, right.)

Do You Remember When...

Otto Charles (O.C.) Cluss, born in 1889 in St. Louis, Missouri, started his lumber company in 1918 on South Pennsylvania Avenue in Uniontown. Cluss was elected president and general manager, positions he would hold for forty years. Mr. Cluss had an important role in bringing the Penn State Fayette Campus to the area; he served as chairman of the fundraising campaign for the first campus building. His sons, John and Charles, and their brother-in-law C.J. Barnes, established the O.C. Cluss Lumber as a major supplier of construction and building materials in western Pennsylvania during the 1960s. They added a second yard in Greensburg in 1986 and a third in Aliquippa. *Pro Sales* magazine ranked Cluss Lumber as the 72nd largest lumber and building supplier in the country. O.C. Cluss continues as a privately held business, employing 350 people in the tri-state area. Otto Cluss's legacy as a community-minded businessman continues to this day through his sons Charles, Chairman of the Board and member of the Fayette County Community Foundation, and John, a Fayette County historian active in preserving our local history. His daughter-in-law Mary Cluss is a member of the Uniontown Public Library Board. (Charles and Mary Cluss collection.)

Teenaged students are awaiting the start of their day at the newly built Redstone High School near Republic. The busses that transported them to the school are quite unlike those that we are accustomed to today and may have been from the Redstone Auto Bus and Taxi Line. Boys and girls from all over Redstone Township attended high school here, and in some years, Luzerne Township, which did not have a high school of its own, sent their secondary students here, too. This practice continued on and off until the fall of 1966 when Brownsville, Redstone and Luzerne townships and Brownsville Borough formed

the Brownsville Area School District. The Redstone High School building was demolished in the summer of 2006. (Bill and Lois Wolfersberger collection.)

In early February of 1935 second semester classes began at the Penn State Center in downtown Uniontown. Both day and evening classes were offered at the former Central School Building. Convocation was held on February 5 for the sixty-nine original students who had successfully completed their first semester at the new junior college. The Penn State Center would operate here until 1945. Among those enrolled in the college's first classes was W. Ralston McGee, who would later become a doctor and serve as a Fayette County coroner. (Franklin V. LaCava collection.)

Do You Remember When...

The Breakneck or Finley Furnace was built along Breakneck Creek near Connellsville by Miller, Rogers and Paul in 1818 but was no longer in use after 1838. The site of this furnace, now under water, is approximately 3.2 miles east of Pittsburgh Street. Stones from this furnace were used to build the dam at Breakneck. (Rev. Peter Malik collection.)

This is a rare photograph of Lemont Furnace in North Union Township. Lemont Furnace was one of the larger furnaces and used Fayette County coke and iron ore. The furnace went into blast for the production of iron in 1876. The earlier stone-stack furnaces were replaced by the kind at Lemont Furnace. Dunbar, Fairchance and Oliphant also had this type of furnace. (Mick Gallis collection.)

The Wharton Iron Furnace is one of Fayette County's best examples of an early blast furnace. The furnace built by Andrew Stewart was in operation from 1839 to about 1873. Cannonballs were manufactured here during the Civil War. Our county was one of the first to produce iron from ore west of the Alleghenies. The furnace is located on a beautiful parcel of land in Wharton Township two miles off Route 40 on the second road past the historical Mt. Summit Inn. This scenic mountain area is a great place to enjoy on a cool summer day. (Mick Gallis collection.)

Semet Solvay Ovens, Dunbar, Pa.

The Semet-Solvay Coke Works was owned by the Dunbar Furnace Company. They opened in 1895 with 110 by-product coke ovens. Unlike beehive ovens, the by-product ovens also made tar, fertilizer, light oil and phenol, making the coking process more profitable. These ovens were based on a European invention and introduced in America in 1887, although the first recorded production date was 1893. The Dunbar ovens were the second by-product ovens built in the United States. The products turned out by these ovens were normally used in the steel industry, therefore the ovens were usually constructed near steel plants unlike the ones in Dunbar that were built close to the coal source. (Author's collection, top left. Betty O. Wilson collection, middle left.)

Beeson and Hogsett owned the Dunbar Furnace, which employed about 325 workers in 1874. Dunbar had coke manufacturing and ample timber, ore, limestone and water resources, all beneficial for a successful iron furnace company. The Dunbar Furnace was the first in our state to use a Whitwell hot-blast stove in which the blast is heated as it passes through firebrick walls. Pig iron bars can be seen next to the tracks in this photograph. E.C. Pechin managed the

Dunbar Furnace and developed a laboratory for the scientific analysis of iron ore. The Dunbar Furnace turned out 13,494 tons of iron in 1875. Dunbar was building its reputation as a "Furnace Town." (Mick Gallis collection.)

At one time about 15,000,000 board feet of lumber was cut and sold in Fayette County. This natural resource came in handy when lumber was needed for the mines and the workers' houses. Timber was transported by horse and wagon from the forests to the towns. (Kathy Smitley collection. Uniontown Public Library collection, middle.)

The Charles Eggers Company, founded in 1894, was the first lumber company in this section of the state to replace the horse-drawn wagon with delivery by motor vehicle and was the first in southwestern Pennsylvania to use electricity to operate mill machinery. The business was situated very close to Redstone Creek and was subject to flooding. (Janice Mancuso collection.)

Skilled stonemasons erected the ovens out of stone and shaped them into hives with bricks that may have been manufactured at the Fairchance Fire Brick Company, the Layton Fire Brick Company near Dawson or other nearby brick manufacturers. During the early 1900s, there were mines of soft clay and flint clay in Fayette County. The "fire clays" mined from the Westmoreland County line to southwest Fairchance were used to manufacture paving brick and firebrick. (William G. Brown collection.)

The Gates Mine was south of Middle Run on the Monongahela River in German Township and served by the Monongahela Valley Railroad. This shaft mine was established by the American Coke Company and opened in 1899 but was acquired by H. C. Frick two years later. The mine once employed 450 workers. There were two major explosions at the Gates Mine. The first in 1922 injured many and claimed several lives; there were no deaths but many were hurt during another explosion in 1924. (Author's collection.)

Constructing coke ovens was a year-round process. Working conditions were poor and both men and mules worked long hours, even building these beehive ovens in the dead of winter. (William G. Brown collection.)

Do You Remember When...

In both 1891 and 1894, Fayette County's organized coal miners were involved in bitter strikes. As a result of the vicious strike of 1922, the union won a wage increase for the miners, but only after a bitter battle with the mine owners resulted in massive mine shutdowns and the eviction of nearly 90% of the miners from their patch homes. Some families were forced to live in tents or even in the coke ovens. In June of 1933 the miners in this county reorganized and for the first time in fifty years were acknowledged by the UMWA. The goal of the organization is understanding, tolerance and fair dealing with the workforce of the community. (Author's collection.)

Abraham Overholt first produced whiskey at his farm in West Overton. Due to an increase in the popularity of Overholt's "Old Farm" whiskey, he established the Overholt Distillery on the Youghiogheny River at Broad Ford, Dunbar Township. The complex manufactured Monongahela and A. Overholt & Company Pure Rye Whiskey. During the early 1900s about sixty-five thousand gallons of whiskey was produced daily. During Prohibition, the Overholt Distillery had special permission to produce whiskey for "medicinal purposes." Overholt's grandson, Abraham Overholt Tinstman joined the distillery business and later became the president of the Mt. Pleasant and Broad Ford Railroad Co., which eventually was sold to the B & O Railroad. (Author's collection.)

Henry Clay Frick, son of John and Elizabeth Overholt Frick and grandson of Abraham Overholt, began his career as a clerk and bookkeeper at the Overholt Distillery. Frick went on to become one of the wealthiest men in America due to his business savvy and ventures in coal and coke. The Frick Coke Company dominated the Connellsville Coal and Coke Region. While the laborers and their families were barely surviving, Frick was living like a king, spending millions on mansions, vacations and expensive art works. H.C. Frick hungered for more wealth and used ruthless union-busting methods; for this, most coal miners and business competitors shared a hatred for him. Only Frick could print his own money, used for his Frick mining communities. The bills were the same color and size as U. S. paper currency. An assassination attempt was made on Frick at this office at Fifth Avenue in Pittsburgh. Fayette County advisor and attorney Philander Knox was with Frick when he survived being shot and stabbed by a Russian anarchist. (Uniontown Public Library collection.)

Do You Remember When...

The General Chemical Company at Newell was situated near the Pittsburgh and Lake Erie Railroad along the Monongahela River. The plant began its operation in 1906 and eventually had 285 employees. Thirty single-family two-bay houses were constructed in 1910 along Second, Third and Fayette streets to accommodate the workers. The plant manufactured chemicals, some of which were used to pickle steel, a process that removed the iron oxide scale formed during steel production. (Mick Gallis collection.)

This worker is drawing coke from one of the ovens in the Connellsville region. Coke weighs only a fraction of an equal amount of coal because the coking process has burned off all the coal by-products leaving pieces of almost pure carbon, the fuel of the steel-making process. (Mick Gallis collection.)

The first coke drawn from a beehive coke oven in Fayette County was in 1833. The oven, designed by a man named Nichols, was built in what is now Connellsville. The early beehive coke ovens were much smaller than the ovens that were built in later years. Between 1876 and 1882, the number of beehive coke ovens increased from 3,000 to 8,400. By 1907 there were 23,857 coke ovens in operation in the Connellsville coke region. (William G. Brown collection.)

W.J. Rainey Company's Royal coke plant in Redstone Township was one of the most modern and best-equipped plants in the region. The plant was near the present-day Pleasant View church, one mile northeast of Uniontown. The mineshaft was 400-feet deep and tapped into a vein of coal nine-feet thick. The tipple towered 138 feet above the ground, one of the highest in the coke region. Two hundred rectangular or Mitchell coke ovens were built here. The smoke from the ovens seldom bothered the residents of 100 six-room company houses built on

an elevation overlooking the plant. The Rainey Company used a Morgan mining machine that could dig and load coal, an experimental technique in 1908. Rainey officials said this machine could do the work of sixty men. Even during the early 1900s companies were hoping to replace the laborers with machinery. (Sandra L. Michotte collection.)

A horse or mule pulling a wooden wagon was the primary method to transport coal to the surface. The miner hand loaded the coal then led his buddy to the surface. The only light available was sunlight or a carbide lamp on the miner's cap. Because they were constantly in darkness, many of the mules and ponies went blind. (Mick Gallis collection.)

The W. J. Rainey Coal Company proudly displayed this three-ton block of coal on a platform near the courthouse during Uniontown's Centennial Celebration in 1896. The huge chunk was decorated with flags and bunting, and an armed guard stood watch so that no one could chip a piece from the coal as a souvenir. Fayette County had some of the best coal in America. (Walter "Buzz" Storey collection.)

Do You Remember When...

Chapter 5
On the Move and Bridging Gaps

Uniontown's first trolley terminal moved from Main Street to Penn Street in 1930. The Penn Street terminal is now the site of the present day Laurel Business Institute. The West Penn inter-urban trolley system expanded from Uniontown to Dunbar, then to Connellsville, on to Mt. Pleasant, and finally into Greensburg. Stops were also made at Brownsville, Hopwood, Masontown, Fairchance and many of the small coal company towns. The streetcars ran every thirty minutes from 5:30 a.m. to 8:30 p.m., then every hour until 11:30 p.m. The cars ran an hour later on Sundays. (Uniontown Public Library collection.)

This automobile just left the city limits headed east along the National Road. The view in the background is spectacular. After passing through Hopwood, the climb will be steep and the driver may need to stop to cool down his engine a few times before he reaches the Summit. (Uniontown Public Library collection.)

The Summit House was an inn and a favorite gathering place along the National Road for many years. Folks could enjoy the fresh cool mountain air while relaxing in wooden rockers on the porch. Later, a more modern resort called the Summit Inn would take its place. (Uniontown Public Library collection.)

J. Buell Snyder (dressed in a white suit and shoes) attended a sunrise ceremony with other dignitaries at Fort Necessity in July of 1937. Also present were Judge Horatio Dumbauld and Rev. T. Dunn of St. John's Church, along with veterans from several wars and leaders of military organizations. Snyder was a member of the board of education in Perry Township and a school principal. He served as a U. S. Representative from Pennsylvania from March 4, 1933 until his death. While serving as the chairman of the House Appropriations Committee, Snyder was credited with obtaining the funding necessary to conduct vital secret experiments that resulted in the atomic bomb. He was a pioneer in the development of the interstate highway system. J. Buell Snyder was a friend and advisor to Gen. George Marshall. Upon hearing of Snyder's death Marshall said, "The army has lost a strong friend." (Mick Gallis collection.)

This gentleman is riding his bicycle past the Fayette Courthouse on East Main Street in 1896. He may have been one of the entrants in the bicycle race during the Uniontown's Centennial Celebration. During the 1890s bicycles, trains and horses were all common means of travel. (Walter "Buzz" Storey collection.)

A train chugs along over the Youghiogheny River at Ohiopyle with a huge cargo of coal. The Western Pennsylvania Railroad Company built this bridge high above the river in 1911. The concrete piers each measure about one hundred and ten feet high. The Youghiogheny appeared rather calm on the day this photograph was taken around 1920. (Author's collection.)

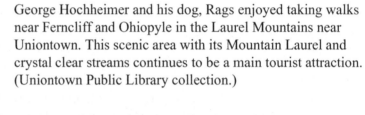

George Hochheimer and his dog, Rags enjoyed taking walks near Ferncliff and Ohiopyle in the Laurel Mountains near Uniontown. This scenic area with its Mountain Laurel and crystal clear streams continues to be a main tourist attraction. (Uniontown Public Library collection.)

George M. Hochheimer was a frequent visitor at the Ohiopyle Hotel during the early 1900s. He is shown here sitting on the cement base of the magnificent fountain in front of the hotel. The Uniontown businessman was born in 1879. In 1915 he opened Hochheimer & Company. He and his wife Anna were kind and charitable and his business associates had the utmost respect for him. Mr. Hochheimer helped many of the community's younger generation to achieve their educational aspirations. (Uniontown Public Library collection.)

People traveling by horseback on the National Road needed a place to rest their horses after a long, hot, tiresome trip over the Summit Mountains. In the early days of 1900 folks could get a bite to eat at the Watering Trough and some refreshing mountain spring water for their horses. In later years, bewildered travelers with overheated automobile radiators were thankful for the spring at the Watering Trough. (Author's collection.)

A horse drawn trolley is transporting children through the deep woods of our snowy mountains to a one-room schoolhouse. In winter the children were awakened before dawn and dressed in many layers of clothing for their daily ride to school near the Summit Mountain. (Author's collection.)

A snowstorm near Confluence during the early 1900s buried most of the roads in monstrous drifts. Before the days of trucks with snowplows, crews of men had to hand shovel the deep snow off the roads. Almost everyone who has lived in Fayette County has a favorite snowfall story that they enjoy sharing with others. (Author's collection.)

Do You Remember When...

The Searights Tollhouse is one of the last remaining tollhouses along the National Road. The Menallen Township landmark has gone through many changes since it was built in 1835. The most recent transformation was made possible through the efforts of the Fayette County Commissioners, the Pennsylvania Historical and Museum Commission and the

Fayette County Historical Society who serve as the current managers. In this scene we can travel back in time to observe the tollgate keeper collecting a fee from a wagoner traveling along the National Road. (Uniontown Public Library collection.)

Searights Tavern was midway between Uniontown and Brownsville along the National Road. In 1821 contractor William Searight acquired the old stone tavern built by Josiah Frost and employed James Allison to manage the tavern for him. Searights in large gilt letters on a sign on the front of the house attracted wagoners and other travelers along the National Road. Post riders would stop here and take a rest from delivering the documents and mail that was bulging from their saddlebags. Political meetings, dances and other memorable events were held in the tavern during the era when the National Road was flourishing. (Uniontown Public Library collection.)

It is hard to image a trolley filled with passengers swaying back and forth on such narrow tracks high above the ground. Trolley service in Fayette County came to an end in the early 1950s, making way for more modern, but less organized means of travel. (Author's collection.)

Harrison A. Wood was the conductor on this Connellsville-New Haven and Leisenring Street Railway Car. John K. Ewing secured the right-of-way for an electric streetcar from Connellsville to Leisenring in 1890. The opening trip on October 31, 1891 was crowded with curiosity seekers wanting to see the operation of the "first car" in Fayette County. While coming down the hill into New Haven on the return run, the motorman lost control of the car, sliding into a passing freight train at the crossing of the Southwest Pennsylvania Railroad's Possum Run branch. The car spun completely around and the rear end was demolished. Several passengers were hurt with one boy suffering a severe leg injury and one man tragically losing his life. (Curt Lehman collection.)

Betty Lehman, nee Betty O. Wilson, is shown in 1947 standing on the trolley tracks where they cross over from the Catholic Church to the Greenhill bank in Dunbar. Passengers must have felt like they were on a roller coaster rather than a trolley with all the hills and trestles the tracks traversed in hilly southwestern Pennsylvania. Both the trolley and the Pennsylvania Railroad used this trestle that was removed in later years. (Betty O. Wilson collection.)

Do You Remember When...

The Endsley homestead was the oldest residence in Somerfield. This landmark was located beside the old bridge and overlooked the Youghiogheny River. The house was built just before 1818, at about the same time Philip D. Smyth laid out the town. That same year, President James Monroe and his cabinet attended the opening of the Great Crossings Bridge, the bridge that carried Route 40 across the Youghiogheny River. Former state senator James W. Endsley spent the entire 84 years of his life in the old homestead. The future Mrs. Endlsey moved to Somerfield when she was only nine. In the name of progress, all of the buildings in the town were demolished or flooded to make way for the gigantic flood control dam. Most of the residents were resigned to the fact that they had to leave their old homes but at age 83, Mrs. Endsley remained a strenuous objector and said, "It will be the death of me." (*News Standard*.)

This scene is looking along Route 40 in Somerfield. Building a dam across the Youghiogheny necessitated the removal of 150 families, including the entire town of Somerfield with 176 residents and the village of Thomasdale, both in Pennsylvania, and part of Selbysport in Maryland. Two cemeteries had to be moved to higher ground. (Uniontown Public Library collection.)

Do You Remember When...

The Bethelboro area of North Union Township has seen tremendous growth over the years: from one-room school houses, quaint country churches and historical cemeteries to a modern four-lane highway, beautiful housing developments and thriving businesses. It was necessary to either demolish or move the Wilson house in Bethelboro to build the beginning phase of the Route 119 bypass. Some men in the community placed monetary bets on whether or not a house could be successfully picked up and moved but the Wilson house was relocated without any structural damage. (Betty O. Wilson collection.)

The railroad company is evaluating the possibility of laying train tracks in Jefferson Township in 1913 near the property of Stephen Nutt, brother of Captain A.C. Nutt. Jefferson Township was formed out of Washington Township and at one time manufacturing and railroading were the main industries. (Author's collection.)

Do You Remember When...

On December 5, 1925, a "new" White Swan Hotel was dedicated and introduced to the public. During the dedication ceremony, J. Searight Marshall, a descendant of the Brownfield family, expressed that he was pleased to help preserve the traditions at the White Swan and that he hoped future generations would continue to gather at "The sign of the White Swan." Nathaniel Brownfield's children, Thomas Brownfield, Susan Thorndell, Emma Moore and Elma Breading attending the ceremony. (Bettie C. O'Neil collection.)

These lovely ladies are the daughters of Nathaniel D. Brownfield (top right), proprietor of the original White Swan Hotel, and his wife Gulielma Maria Mitchell Brownfield (bottom right). All of these women were over sixty-five years of age when this photograph was taken. In the front from left to right are Emma Moore, Susan Thorndell, Lizzie Prentice and Minerva Hinsey. Elma Breading, Louisa Hadden and Rachel Gray are in the second row. (Uniontown Public Library collection.)

Fayette County's claim to fame is Brownsville's Dunlap Creek Bridge, built in 1836, the oldest existing cast iron bridge in the entire country and listed on the National Register of Historic Places. Building and maintaining bridges has been a major industry in an area with an abundance of streams, creeks, runs and major rivers. (Mick Gallis collection.)

Railroad workers pose with a P&LE locomotive for a picture taken along the National Road in the early 1900s. The Pittsburgh and Lake Erie Railroad first came to the upper Monongahela Valley in 1890 when the company purchased a portion of the McKeesport and Belle Vernon Railroad. The twenty-seven mile section brought the railroad within seven miles of Brownsville. In the distance the old cast iron bridge is visible through the third arch of the modern stone bridge. (David Gratz collection.)

The old covered bridge that once connected Brownsville to West Brownsville was demolished in October of 1910. In September of that year the bridge was closed and residents were forced to cross the river by ferry service. The bridge had stood for over 77 years. The creaky bridge was pulled into the waters of the Monongahela using six large cables attached to the towboat, the Robert Jenkins. Thousands of people witnessed this historical event. (Uniontown Public Library collection.)

The Brownsville, Bridgeport and West Brownsville area pioneered the boat building industry west of the Alleghenies. The first steam boats and paddle boats that navigated on the Monongahela and Ohio Rivers were also built here. Boats and barges filled with bituminous coal were the main river traffic for about 200 years. Most of Fayette County's coal and coke was hauled down the river to Pittsburgh to the steel mills. Boats traveled along the rivers of southwestern Pennsylvania until the railroads became the dominant method of travel and transport. Fayette County's coal and coke industry is now nearly non-existent; its rivers are mainly used for pleasure crafts and drinking water supplies. (Mick Gallis collection.)

The town of New Geneva in Nicholson Township was once named Wilson's Port after Col. George Wilson, a settler from Augusta County, Virginia, and an officer during the French and Indian War. Albert Gallatin later bought the town, renaming it New Geneva. The New Geneva Hotel was located on the main road in the town. It was at the hotel that local dignitaries and the people in the community rolled out the red carpet for the Marquis de Lafayette and honored him for his service to America. (Uniontown Public Library collection.)

J.R. Marshall and Isaac Brownfield once owned the Old Hill House near Cheat Haven in Springhill Township. The two men used the house along the Cheat River as a hotel and campground for friends and family members. As time went on and the coal mining business began to flourish, countryside structures such as this one were torn down and faded away and coal tipples were built upon the sites. (Bettie C. O'Neil collection.)

This is a rare image of the arch on the B&O Railroad near Guyaux, Pennsylvania. This town near Point Marion was named for P. J. Guyaux, Sr., a major landowner and glass manufacturer. He was born in Belgium in 1857 and brought his trade with him to this country. He planned and built the Point Marion window glass plant. (Mick Gallis collection.)

This ten-stall round house, machine house and engine house near Brownsville were all built for efficiency, replacing the outdated original engine house and one-stall building in order to better perform the necessary repairs on a fleet of twelve locomotives. The Bridgeport Mine river tipple can be seen over the round house. The nearby Bridgeport Coke Works opened in 1900 with 100 rectangular ovens and was owned by the River Coal Company and later purchased by the H.C. Frick Coke Company. Transporting coal and coke by trains along the rivers was at its peak during this time in Fayette

County making a modern repair station and train yard such as this one in great demand. A fire destroyed this roundhouse, machine shop and engine house in 1916. (David Gratz collection.)

This train wreck occurred very close to the homes at Mount Sterling, south of Masontown. The ground rumbled as if there had been an earthquake as cars loaded with coal overturned and derailed. The residents ran from their homes to see what had caused the booming and screeching sounds in their neighborhood. The tremendous force of the wreck caused several cars to twist and break apart, spilling and tossing coal everywhere. (David Gratz collection.)

The Reed Tire Shop was on Liberty Street in Uniontown's East End during the 1950s. Arthur Reed was the owner of the re-capping tire service that was located next to his brother-in-law's business, Rudy's Body Shop. Neighborhood businesses like these have almost become extinct. Tire shop owner Arthur Reed, who is the author's

uncle, is standing to the right of his neighbor, Herman Thomas. (Carol Dutko Marshaus collection.)

In 1939 Stone & Work Service Station at 392 E. Main Street was owned and managed by Charles Stone and C. Robert Work. During the 1940s Charles M. Stone, Wendell A. Stone and William H. Stone were owners and managers of the full-service station now called Stone & Company. Pictured is Lyale Linwood Hahn of Continental I who walked to and from his job at Stone & Company for about five years following his retirement from the Continental I Mine where he fired the boilers. In the mid 1950s, the Polk's City Directory shows that the station changed ownership and was known as Gordon Gulf Service Station, managed by Bernard Gordon of Brownsville. (Mark Bubonovich collection.)

Edgar E. Strickler was the owner and manager of the Standard Gas and Service Station at 92 West Fayette Street during the 1930s. Only automobile-related services and items were sold in the early stations: batteries, oil, lube jobs, and tire patching. Gas sold at twelve cents a gallon. Friendly attendants dressed in neatly pressed uniforms wanted to tend to our automobile's every need. They checked the level of the oil, the water in the radiator, and the air pressure in the tires and then washed the windows, all at no charge. (*News Standard*, 1933.)

Katherine M. Carr (front) is standing by her airplane at the Connellsville Airport in the 1960s with Harriet 'Tuffy" Call, her flight instructor and former WWII WASP. "Kay" Carr, wife of Judge Philip O. Carr, had earned her pilot's license, a rare thing for a woman at that time. Tuffy and her husband, General Lance Call, lived nearby with their two children and ran the airport and the Summit Flying School based there. At one time the Army used the airport, which was one of the chain of defense ports in our area protecting industrial Pittsburgh during war times. (Joan Carr collection.)

In April of 1936, the Sun Racer, a TWA airliner, crashed near Laurel Caverns, about four miles behind the Summit and four miles from Haydentown. The plane was en route from Newark, N.J. to Pittsburgh when it got off course. The wing struck a tree and nosedived into the virgin forest, cracking into pieces. Eleven persons died and three were injured. Heroic stewardess Nellie Granger dragged herself two miles to get to a telephone. Doctors, ambulances, nurses, state police and volunteers rushed to the disaster scene along the Coroner Baltz. Several other plane crashes have occurred in Fayette County. (William R. Wilson collection.)

Do You Remember When...

During a flood in Fayette City during the early 1900s, the townspeople helped the passengers from this train safely to higher ground. The tracks were laid a little to close to the Monongahela River, which is known to rise above its banks during a heavy rainy season. (Author's collection.)

Percy Dillingham Hagan operated the Fayette Supply Company at Oliver and managed and owned the Hagan Grocery on Morgantown Street. Mr. Hagan also organized and supervised the Hagan Taxicab Company, later known as the White Line Cab & Transfer Company. The local rail service transported goods and supplies to his businesses and his grocery store. Percy D. Hagan, one of Fayette County's most diversified businessmen, was born in Allegheny County and married Laura Carothers of Uniontown. He passed away July 1, 1924, at his home near Braddock's Park. (Bettie C. O'Neil collection.)

One of Fayette County's abundant natural resources, timber was handy during the coal and coke boom when there was a need for houses for coal miners' families and lumber for the mines. Timber was transported early on by horse and wagon from the thick forest to the towns. At one time some 15,000,000 board feet of lumber was cut and sold in Fayette County. (William G. Brown collection.)

Do You Remember When...

The first bridge over the Youghiogheny River was a wooden toll bridge built in 1800. Wooden bridges were easily swept away by high waters and floods. A five span steel truss bridge replaced other bridges that had been built over the river. This Connellsville suspension bridge, strong and impressively designed, was better suited for the increasingly heavier traffic crossing over one the major waterways of Fayette County. (Mick Gallis collection.)

This is a partial view of Dickerson Run and Dawson looking northeast. In 1881 the citizens of the community organized the Dawson Bridge Company with well-known resident James "Big Jim" Cochran as its president, and built this bridge spanning the Youghiogheny River here in 1883. Youghiogheny may have been derived from a Native American term that meant rough and fast moving water. (Mick Gallis collection.)

Railroad service between Connellsville and Uniontown commenced in 1860. In 1871 the railroad was completed from Connellsville to Cumberland, opening up trade and travel opportunities. A train is about to make a stop at the Connellsville Train Station in this scenic image of the town during 1952. The iron bridge can be seen off in the distance. (Rev. Peter Malik collection.)

Do You Remember When...

The Albion Hotel was one of the five original hotels in Fairchance. As any other thriving community and small industrial center, Fairchance had the need for hotels that could accommodate groups of people such as commercial travelers and railroad employees. During the coal mining strike of 1922, the Pennsylvania State Police were stationed at the Albion. Their horses were kept in a large stable in the rear of the property. The Albion Hotel stood as a reminder of the past until it was destroyed by fire in the 1980s. (Janice Mancuso collection.)

This image of an intersection in Connellsville taken during the early 1900s shows the importance that the railroad played in the town. This is clearly an area of commerce and trade, not a residential area. The train tracks are part of the Pennsylvania Railroad, completed in 1876. (Uniontown Public Library collection.)

Judge Nathaniel Ewing arranged to have the bricks molded and fired in a kiln directly on site when he built the Mount Washington Tavern around 1829. The tavern was once part of the Good Intent Stage Line and on one morning served breakfast to seventy-two stage passengers. In 1840 Judge Ewing sold the tavern to James Sampey. Travel along the National Road was at its peak during this time. People traveling by coach or wagon in need of overnight accommodations would tend to the needs of their own horses, pay for their bedroll, and choose a meal from a selection that typically included boiled smoked ham, boiled mutton, roast beef, fried speckled

trout, fried chicken, fried potatoes, mashed pumpkin, cakes, pies, cheese and coffee. (Uniontown Public Library collection.)

Chapter 6
Faces and Places

Morrell in Dunbar Township was founded in the year 1880 and was named for Daniel J. Morrell of Johnstown. The town of Morrell, also known as Sitka, was once owned by the Cambria Iron Company. Edmund Trimbath, a successful long time merchant in Morrell, opened his store during the 1880s. At one time there were 400 coke ovens in operation in Morrell, and many laborers worked and resided there, contributing to the success of Trimbath's business. It is believed that this early 1900s photograph was taken during a Memorial Day celebration. (Curt Lehman collection.)

Crowds cheered as the Point Marion Bridge opened in July of 1909. The Penn Bridge Company had the contract to construct the bridge. The citizens of Point Marion combined the nation's birthday with the dedication of the bridge. The celebration opened before dawn with cannon fire, marking a memorable day in Point Marion's history. (Mick Gallis collection.)

This is a picturesque image of Point Marion, a borough in the most southern part of the county at the junction of the Cheat and Monongahela rivers. John Sadler founded the town about 1843. Point Marion had retail stores, lumber and mill works and a bottling plant. Several factories manufactured convex glass and window glass. Another primary industry was loading and shipping sand and gravel. Point Marion was a vital river port. (Author's collection.)

F.P. Morgan of Uniontown took this photograph long before the days of automobile travel and before the B&O Railroad was built to Pt. Marion. From left to right: Miss May Schnatterly, Miss Elma M. Brownfield, Mrs. Isaac B. Brownfield, Ewing B. Brownfield, Isaac B. Brownfield, Joseph R. Marshall, and J. Searight Marshall. This was country living at its best. The visitors would relax by a campfire and sing a few songs accompanied by fiddlers and guitar players. (Bettie C. O'Neil collection.)

Fairchance was founded about 1870 and incorporated as a borough March 7, 1889. It is located six miles south of Uniontown. At one time both the B&O and the Monongahela railroads passed through the borough. Two trolley lines also provided transportation: the West Penn Railway and the Fairchance & Smithfield. (Mick Gallis collection.)

Fairchance residents prospered from the many industries and businesses that once supplied goods to areas around Fayette County. Coke, coal, glassware, bricks, explosives, lumber, building supplies, as well as products made at various mills were produced here in Fairchance. Early on the town profited from the iron furnace industry. This magnificent home on Main Street with its ornate iron fence was typical of those that were built by the affluent businessmen in the community. (Author's collection.)

Masontown was once referred to as Germantown because the area was first settled by people of German descent. Masontown experienced a boom in housing and commerce during the coal and coke era. Charming well-built homes line a main road in the borough in this photo taken during the early 1900s. (Mick Gallis collection.)

Do You Remember When...

Brownsville's business district was filled to capacity during the 1920s and 30s. A branch store of the I.N. Hagan Ice Cream Company was situated on Bridge and High streets. The Strand Theatre on Market Street was a favorite entertainment spot. Wise's Department Store, Kaufman's, David Furniture, G.C. Murphy's 5 & 10 Cent Store, and Kirk Shoes and Hosiery were part of a great shopping mecca. Shopping downtown was quite a different experience than today's mall shopping. The ladies would have on their finest dresses, young men would wear their knickers and men would dress in their best suits and hats. (Author's collection, top. Uniontown Public Library collection, middle.)

Fayette City is located along the Monongahela River twelve miles from Brownsville. The borough was first named Freeport, and then Cookstown after Col. Edward Cook, a friend to George Washington. At one time this riverfront town had three glass factories. Coal mining was a major industry here. The town was also known for its many retail stores. Some of the buildings in Fayette City are reminiscent of the Civil War era and others of the Victorian period. (Author's collection.)

Do You Remember When...

James R. Barnes made his fortune in the coal business. Fayette County was experiencing a boom in the coal and coke industry, and some of the speculators in the coal lands became millionaires almost overnight. Barnes had his permanent home in Uniontown on East Main Street, but he built a spectacular mansion as his summer home at the foot of Mount Summit in Hopwood. His estate had an in-ground pool, fishponds and fountains. One building with great wooden floors was so large that in later years it was turned into a dance palace. The Hopwood estate was known as Martha's Place. Barnes took advantage of Fayette County's resources to build Martha's Place, using high quality lumber taken from the stands of virgin forest in nearby Lick Hollow. Martha's Place was built to be enjoyed by family, friends and the community and continues to attract the attention of those traveling along the National Road. (Uniontown Public Library collection.)

German D. Hair built many substantial and impressive-looking buildings along the National Road including his own stone tavern in Hopwood. German D. Hair, born in July of 1790, married Rebecca Brownfield in 1809. Hair was a classmate and great admirer of James Buchanan. (Uniontown Public Library collection.)

Do You Remember When...

This is an early street scene in New Salem, which was named after Salem, Massachusetts. The village located in Menallen Township was once called Muttontown, supposedly because the whereabouts of many stolen sheep were traced here. David Arnold laid out the town in 1799, but there were previous owners of this village site. (Uniontown Public Library collection.)

This is the Leckrone Passenger and Freight Station. Freight was received at the B & O interchange track and can be seen in the building in the background built in 1901. Many company towns throughout Fayette County had passenger and freight stations. (David Gratz collection.)

The New Salem passenger station was built in 1903 at a cost of $3,185. The main track was on the bridge above Dunlap's Creek. (David Gratz collection.)

Lida Niccolls Fitzgerald married Prince Victor Theodor Maxmillian Egon Marie Lamoral of Baltavor, Hungary, the Prince of Thurn and Taxis. The Princess of Thurn and Taxis filed numerous lawsuits, including one against the city of Uniontown and another against her daughter-in-law. She also sued her uncle, J.V. Thompson, claiming that he mishandled her investments. (Uniontown Public Library collection.)

Princess Lida Eleanor of Thurn and Taxis poses here with her three sons, Edward Purcell-Fitzgerald and Gerald Purcell-Fitzgerald, and John Purcell-Fitzgerald. The children were the sons of her first husband, Gerald Purcell-Fitzgerald, a wealthy Irish nobleman. During their adulthood, the Fitzgerald sons resided in New York and New Jersey. The Princess and two of her sons are buried at Oak Grove Cemetery. (Uniontown Public Library collection.)

James Veech, a prominent judge, attorney and the author of the local history, *Monongahela of Old*, built this spectacular mansion at 177 South Mt. Vernon Street. The home was shown

on a Uniontown map as early as 1855 and was still standing 110 years later. The Veech mansion later became the home of the prominent Niccolls family of Brownsville. Mr. and Mrs. Niccolls' daughter Lida, aka the Princess of Thurn and Taxis and niece of coal baron J.V. Thompson, would occupy this mansion until her death on December 6, 1965. This distinctive home once held valuable treasures from all over the world, and it is said that Princess Lida had a passion for collecting unusual objects because of her eccentric nature. Her house was torn down to make way for the Mt. Vernon Towers, a modern high-rise apartment building. (Uniontown Public Library collection, middle left. Haky family collection middle right, bottom left.)

Do You Remember When...

Josiah Van Kirk Thompson is best known as a millionaire coal baron and businessman but he was also a devoted family man who enjoyed spending time with friends. Thompson was quite a genealogist during his later years. At one time Thompson owned about 1,800 acres of land in Fayette County. In 1903 he built Oak Hill, a beautiful mansion for his second wife, Hunnie Hawes. Thompson constructed the first and only skyscraper in Uniontown, the First National Bank. He was also one of the first owners of an automobile in the county. Thompson was later forced into bankruptcy and his wife divorced him. Today, his mansion is called Mt. Macrina, one of Fayette County's historical landmarks and a tribute to J.V. Thompson. (A. Patrick Palinni collection, middle, top right.)

George and Anna Watson Hochheimer and friends stopped at the J.V. Thompson estate to rest after walking near the property. They are clad in their best hats and dress clothes. Thompson's Oak Hill mansion can be seen in the background of this early 1900s photograph. (Uniontown Public Library collection.)

Do You Remember When...

Blanche Hawes, a 30-year-old widow and curvaceous beauty met J. V. Thompson at the Waldorf Hotel in New York City. Blanche, now using her nickname "Hunnie," was hoping for someone like Thompson. Hunnie had a small fortune that she had inherited from her first husband. Thompson, a widower in New York on business, was more than approachable and Hunnie asked him to invest the money for her. J.V. quickly turned her money into a half million dollars. Hunnie and Thompson exchanged hundreds of flowery love letters. She and J.V. Thompson had married three months after their meeting. Hunnie began spending J.V.'s money extravagantly. First, they honeymooned for 14 months in Europe and Asia. Thompson spent two million dollars on antiques to fill their new mansion, Oak Hill. Hunnie was eccentric, flamboyant and a showoff, especially when they had parties or went to horse races accompanied by her entire entourage of servants. J.V. was generous, kind and down to earth, finding joy in life's simpler things. Just before J. V. lost most of his fortune, Hunnie packed up her diamonds and moved to New York. She was granted a million dollar settlement. Hunnie, who once resembled a brunette version of Mae West, developed elephantitis as her weight reached 600 pounds. Hunnie donated most of the million dollars to a home for wayward girls, so some good came from her time in power in a small coal and coke town in southwestern Pennsylvania. (A. Patrick Pallini collection.)

This lady and gentlemen are playing a game of tennis at the Thompson estate during the early 1900s while off in the distance a dark cloud of smoke can be seen coming from the coke ovens near a company town. The two images epitomize the great disparity in lifestyles of the people in Fayette County at that time. (A. Patrick Pallini collection.)

Smock was built on the homestead of Mr. and Mrs. Samuel Smock. In the early days there was only a mill and a blacksmith shop, but by around 1910 Smock had three general stores, a clothing and shoe store, a fruit and candy store, a grange hall, a livery and feed stable, an Owl clubroom, a hotel, a barbershop, a blacksmith shop, two telephone exchanges, a PRR Station, a post office, a policeman and its very own doctor. An extensive coking plant owned by H. C. Frick was once on the outskirts of this coal mining village. (Uniontown Public Library collection.)

George Washington once owned the land on which Perryopolis now stands. He held ownership to a tract of 1,643 acres. In his diary, Washington described the land as being as fine as any he had ever seen, with level well-watered land and with a very favorable site for a mill. This picturesque town was laid out in 1814 from a design formulated by Washington. (Mick Gallis collection.)

Dickerson Run was named for Joshua Dickerson, an early settler. Stories tell that he came over the mountains around the 1770s looking for property. The area of Dickerson Run became a mining community during the Connellsville Coal and Coke boom. Good railroads and river travel made it a perfect location for this industry. Early on Dickerson Run was referred to as Galley Town. (Uniontown Public Library collection.)

Do You Remember When...

In 1943 Uniontown Senior High School students Eleanor Ciszek and Legatha Harford organized a scrap drive. Theses young ladies were willing to get a little dirty salvaging metal as part of their patriotic duty during World War II. Men traditionally took on this task; however, since so many young men were sent off to serve our country, women began organizing scrap drives. The metals were melted down to create other items needed for the war. (Uniontown Area School District.)

Lovely Mabel Hahn is standing beside her home at Continental I in South Union Township holding two enormous icicles during a winter freeze in the late 1930s. Both Mabel and her mother, Kate Hahn, worked at the French Cleaners on Mount Vernon Avenue during World War II. Mabel married Nick Bubonovich of Coolspring in 1943. She became a school librarian, and he, a principal in the Laurel Highlands School District. (Mark Bubonovich collection.)

During the height of the coal and coke era, immigrants were coming from Europe to make this their new home, and Fayette County became a melting pot of people from many ethnic backgrounds. These young ladies are the daughters of Vitale and Marie G. Pandolfi Volpe, Italian immigrants. Left to right in front are Angeline (Alicastro), Maude (Harshman), Theresa (Kalamets) and Grace (Strickler). In the second row are Mary (Gionfriddo), Rose (Muccolli), Lucy (Coffini) and Lena (Sante), who is the author's grandmother. The Volpes also had six sons - Anthony, Frank, John, James, Joseph and Louis - for a total of fourteen children. Years ago it was very common for people to raise large families and even take boarders into their small company houses. Vitale Volpe was a coal miner and filled out his draft registration for World War I at the age of 40. (Renee Dutko Mueller collection.)

The H.C. Frick Coal and Coke Company sponsored the erection of a huge arch for the centennial celebration at the corner of Main and Pittsburgh streets in the business section of Connellsville. P.J. Tormay of Trotter, C.B. Franks of Leisenring, and R.C. Beerbower of Davidson supervised the building of the great arch made of coal and coke picked by hand by coal miners from the three plants named. The entire community was awestruck by the arch that was decorated with white lights and cost $1,000 to build. Bunting and flags decorated nearly every home and building in Connellsville and the children of the community enjoyed the festivities. (Author's collection.)

Mrs. Franklin D. Roosevelt was served lunch at the David Day home in Penn Craft, Luzerne Township, when she visited the WPA settlement on November 29, 1937. Built on land owned by Quakers, Penn Craft was part of the federal project to help displaced coal mining families start their own communities and was administered by the American Friends Service Committee. Mrs. Roosevelt chatted with a group of young people from the community. The First Lady was touring the coal mining towns of Fayette County. (Author's collection.)

Do You Remember When...

West Main Street in Connellsville was filled with prosperous businesses and Victorian-style homes in 1905. Shown here are the Connellsville Courier office and Joseph L. Stader's Furniture and Undertaking business. Connellsville was planning a great centennial celebration to be held in 1906. This busy town along the Youghiogheny River was one of the wealthiest districts in America due to the success of the coal and coke industry. (*Artwork of Fayette County.*)

Market Street in Brownsville was one of the busiest sections in the commercial district of the town in 1906. Brownsville had tremendous wealth as businesses were flourishing and the coal mining industry was booming. People crowded the streets along with their horses and buggies. The need for banking institutions grew. The Monongahela Bank as seen here was an early institution that relocated to Market Street around 1873. (*Artwork of Fayette County.*)

On their way to a favorite place to play, these daredevil children perched themselves on a steep railing near the river in Brownsville to have their pictures taken. (Author's collection.)

Do You Remember When...

Colonel A.D. Boyd once owned this house at 71 S. Pennsylvania Avenue. The façade of this elegant building has gone through many changes over the years and is almost unrecognizable today when compared to older photographs, such as this one. Several prominent families have resided here. Judge Harry A. Cottom purchased the home around 1922. Mr. Henry L. Charlton, President of the Richmond Radiator Company bought the home around 1945. During the 1950s, Dr. Ralston McGee purchased the home. The residence was later converted into the Oats Funeral Home and is now Kezmarsky's Funeral Home. (Margaret Cottom Young collection.)

Thomas Baird Graham was born in 1833, the son of Hugh Graham, builder of Friendship Hill. T.B. Graham lived for many years in the mansion house on the family homestead in Menallen Township. This land was one of the few properties along the National Road that continued to be owned by the descendants of the original patent except for a time when Andrew Stewart resided here. T.B. Graham was admitted to the Fayette County Bar but went to practice law in Pittsburgh. He later returned to the family property and to his Fayette County roots. T.B. Graham was an excellent writer who published articles for various newspapers. Graham died in 1921. (Uniontown Public Library collection.)

The Peoples' Line boat company had been in operation only a few months with their boats, the Elector and Chieftain, when the company was incorporated under an act by the Assembly on February 21, 1868. Their corporate title became the Pittsburgh, Brownsville and New Geneva Packet Company. The boats made daily trips between Pittsburgh and New Geneva on the Monongahela River. The sheer volume of early river transport and passenger travel would astonish today's river buffs and enthusiasts. (Uniontown Public Library collection.)

Rustic wooden bridges were built over many creeks and ponds as a convenience; today they are more often constructed as an attractive landscaping feature. This family is fishing together from a sturdy looking log bridge. (Author's collection.)

White Rocks, a mountain outcropping near Fairchance, will always be associated with Polly Williams, who was tragically pushed to her death here in 1810. However, the White Rocks has been enjoyed by many for its natural beauty. For years, students, vacationers and families on outings have selected this spot from which to view the spectacular countryside. The enormous boulders here have always been a major focal point. These young ladies and men are only pretending to be smoking as a friend photographs them. (Uniontown Public Library collection.)

William Dean Blacka was born in 1844 in Bridgeport, now part of Brownsville. His parents were from England. William was only 16 years old when he entered the military in 1862 to fight in the Civil War. It was quite common then to enlist at a young age. After the Civil War William Blacka moved to the oil fields of Greene County where he worked for two years. He married Barbara Ann Wilkinson. (Betty O. Wilson collection.)

William Blacka moved to Pechin in Dunbar and lived there for about 40 years. He was highly respected and served on the coroner's jury after the 1890 Hill Farm Mine disaster. William was a member of the GAR Post #163 at Dunbar. He is seen here with two of his grandchildren. William Blacka passed away on October 31, 1918, during the influenza epidemic. (Betty O. Wilson collection.)

The Mount Braddock Coronet Band of Dunbar performed at many parades, picnics and social and patriotic events in and around Dunbar during the late 1800s and early 1900s. Each band member owned his own instrument and attended regular practices. Residents looked forward to the spirited songs and dance routines presented by the band. (Kathy Smitley collection.)

Do You Remember When...

124

This is a unique opportunity to view the trolley traveling close to the intersection of Connellsville and Coolspring Streets. People on board were heading into the city by way of East Main Street at the five corners on the East End of town. For most, the street car was the only way folks could travel from the coal mining villages into the city. It must have been quite a thrill to pass the Fayette County Courthouse and the stores during Uniontown's heyday in the early 1900s. (Uniontown Public Library collection.)

This is a summertime view of the family home and porch of Rev. Asa Waters, superintendent of the Jumonville Soldiers' Orphan School. The home with a touch of Victorian elegance was probably newly built at this time around the late 1890s. The ladies could be family members or perhaps teachers at the school. (Uniontown Public Library collection.)

The exquisite white-tailed deer are predominant in our mountain area. A large buck in Pennsylvania can weigh over 200 pounds. Pennsylvania Governor Lawrence signed a bill in October of 1959 adopting the white-tailed deer as Pennsylvania's official state animal. In the winter the coats of the deer become heavier and turn a grayish brown color with flecks of white. These graceful young fawns resemble pinto ponies against the snowy scenery. (Author's collection.)

These two gentlemen are hoping to attract the attention of a young lady near the stately Whyel Chapel at Jumonville. They have chosen the perfect setting for the hydrangeas that are in bloom in the mountains of Fayette County. The lady is most likely a teacher who spent most of her day caring for the children at the Soldier's Orphan School there. (Uniontown Public Library collection.)

Selected Bibliography

Dunbar, the Furnace Town, 1883-1983. Centennial Book Committee, 1983.

Ellis, Franklin. *History of Fayette County, Pennsylvania with Biographical Sketches of Many of Its Pioneers and Prominent Men*. Philadelphia, PA: L.H. Everts & Co., 1882.

Fairchance Through The Years. The Fairchance History Committee, 1989.

The Genius of Liberty. Uniontown, PA. "The Centennial, A Grand Success From Beginning to End." July 9, 1896.

Hadden, James. *A History of Uniontown, the County Seat of Fayette County Pennsylvania*. Uniontown, PA: 1913.

Hart, J. Percy. *Hart's History and Directory of the Three Towns*. Cadwallader, PA: 1904.

Korson, George. *Coal Dust on the Fiddle, songs and stories of the bituminous industry*. Philadelphia, PA: University Press. 1943.

Leonelli, Victoria Dutko. *Around Uniontown*. Charlestown, SC: Arcadia Publishing, 2003.

Maher, Regis M., M.D. *Patches of History...* Dunbar, PA: Stefano's Printing, 1999.

McClenathan, Edie, Burgess, Coll, and Norton. *Centennial History of the Borough of Connellsville, Pennsylvania*, 1806-1906.Columbus, Ohio: Champlin Press, 1906.

News Standard. Uniontown, PA. "Featuring Activities of Uniontown and Vicinity." April 30, 1933.

Oak Hill, Past and Present. Students of the Advanced Placement American History Class, Laurel Highlands Sr. High School, Visual Communications Department, James Kennedy, James Tobal and William Simpson, Instructors. Uniontown, PA: 1980.

O'Hanlon-Lincoln, Ceane. *County Chronicles A Vivid Collection of Fayette County, Pennsylvania Histories*. Chicora, PA: Mechling Bookbindery, 2004.

Storey, Walter J. "Buzz." *Stories of Uniontown and Fayette County*. Herald Standard/ Uniontown Newspapers, Inc. and Stefano's Printing, 1993.

Uniontown Newspapers, Inc. Uniontown, PA.

Index

Made in the USA
Monee, IL
20 December 2019